LIFE AND TEACHING *of the* MASTERS OF THE FAR EAST

VOLUME 6

by

Baird T. Spalding

DeVorss Publications
Camarillo, California

Life and Teaching of the Masters of the Far East, Volume 6
Copyright © 1996 by DeVorss & Company

ISBN: 9780875166988
Library of Congress Control Number: 96-85608
Nineteenth Printing, 2023

Life and Teaching of the Masters of the Far East, 6-Volume Set
ISBN: 9780875165387

DeVorss & Company, Publisher
P.O. Box 1389
Camarillo CA 93011-1389
www.devorss.com

Printed in the United States of America

THE LIFE AND TEACHING
OF THE
MASTERS OF THE FAR EAST
By Baird T. Spalding

Baird T. Spalding, whose name became legend in metaphysical and truth circles during the first half of the 20th century, played an important part in introducing to the Western world the knowledge that there are Masters, or Elder Brothers, who are assisting and guiding the destiny of mankind. The countless numbers of letters that have come in through the years, from all over the world, bear testimony of the tremendous help received from the message in these books.

Partial listing of the contents of the six volumes:

Volume 1: Introduction of the Master Emil — Visit to the "Temple of Silence" — Astral projection — Walking on Water — Visit to the Healing Temple — Emil talks about America — The Snowmen of the Himalayas — New Light on the teachings of Jesus.

Volume II: Visit to the Temple of the Great Tau Cross — Visit with the Master Jesus — Jesus discusses the nature of hell; the nature of God — The Mystery of thought vibrations — Jesus feeds the multitude — An account of a healing experience — Jesus and Buddha visit the group.

Volume III: One of the masters speaks of the Christ consciousness — The nature of cosmic energy — The creation of the planets and the worlds — The trip to Lhasa — Visit at the Temple Pora-tat-sanga — Explaining the mystery of levitation — A doubter becomes convinced of the existence of Jesus.

Volume IV: This material was first presented as "The India Tour Lessons." Each chapter has text for study, as well as guides to teachers for developing and interpreting the material. Among subjects covered: The White Brotherhood — The One Mind — Basis of coming social reorganization — Prana.

Volume V: Material taken from lectures given by Mr. Spalding in California during the last two years of his life. There is also a brief biographical sketch. Partial contents: Camera of past events — Is there a God — The divine pattern — The reality — Mastery over death — The law of supply.

Volume VI: 18 articles by Mr. Spalding, with questions & answers, taken from *Mind Magazine*, 1935-1937, and a contemporary biographical sketch of Spalding. A special section includes rare photos of Spalding, the India Tour group, shipboard accommodations, Calcutta; also letters from the tour and other Spalding memorabilia. Seven manuscripts by Spalding include: Original of the Lord's Prayer — Divine Mastery — Eternal Youth — Rising Out of Limitation — The Power of Thought. A eulogy and reminiscences by friends of Spalding are included.

TABLE OF CONTENTS

A WORD FROM THE PUBLISHER

OVER MANY years and many moves — from downtown Los Angeles to Eagle Rock to Santa Monica to Marina del Rey — DeVorss & Company was long in possession of ten cartons of materials relating to Baird T. Spalding, author of the immensely successful *Life and Teaching of the Masters of the Far East.* Because it was supposed that the cartons held nothing but proofs, printers' correspondence, memos, receipts, and other purely clerical materials relating to the initial printing and subsequent reprinting of the five volumes over the years, they remained dilapidated and unvisited, covered with a heavy layer of dust in a remote corner of DeVorss' huge warehouse.

In May of 1990, prompted by curiosity and hopeful that they might hold something of greater interest — even of importance — I moved the cartons to my office, emptied them, and began the slow process of sorting through their contents. To be sure, there was a preponderance of uninteresting, purely clerical, material. But to my delight there was also much else, including biographical material, letters to and from Spalding, manuscripts, typescripts, documents, photographs, correspondence from the 1935-36 India Tour party, Spalding's personal effects found at the motel in Arizona where he died, and pages from the long-defunct *Mind Magazine*, published by DeVorss for a decade beginning in 1929, to which Spalding contributed numerous articles between 1935 and 1937 accompanied by the question-and-answer format with which readers of Volume 5 are familiar.

The years following the discovery of these precious materials saw the slow process of reviewing and cataloguing them, then newly storing them, this time in appropriate files, affording access for further research, including the compilation of this volume. Through the friendly cooperation of the Philosophical Research Society in Los Angeles and the New York Public Library, neither of which had a complete set, I was able to assemble a complete record of the contributions by Spalding to *Mind Magazine*, for which the reader now has only to turn to the pages of this book.*

Three years to the month before the discovery of these materials, DeVorss & Company was in receipt of the only communication it has ever had from someone purporting to have information about Baird T. Spalding. (All of our efforts, before and since, to find persons with knowledge of Spalding have been unavailing, serving to reinforce the sense that, even in his lifetime, he was an elusive figure, despite his also having had a wide circle of friends and acquaintances — just one of the many paradoxes surrounding this almost mythical man.) In her communication, Ms Lois Binford Proctor shared the recollections of the late Dr. Neva Dell Hunter of the Quimby Center at Alamogordo, New Mexico, "who knew Baird Spalding very

*In 1986 a fire at the Los Angeles Public Library destroyed that institution's holdings of a complete file of *Mind Magazine*.

well and told me of her experiences with him." We are pleased to share these experiences, with the kind permission of Ms Proctor.

Readers familiar with Volume 5 of *Life and Teaching of the Masters of the Far East* will recall the eulogy of Baird Spalding spoken by Douglas DeVorss, Spalding's publisher, at the memorial service held on Sunday, March 22, 1953, at Carr Mortuary Chapel in Tempe, Arizona. We here include the other eulogy given on this occasion, spoken by Spalding's friend David Bruton. The two talks should be read in conjunction with each other, as indicated by the order of Mr. Bruton's remarks.

Volume 6 of *Life and Teaching of the Masters of the Far East* complements the preceding five volumes and consists, then, of the following elements:

1. Articles and Questions & Answers, all by Spalding, from *Mind Magazine*.
2. A new biographical sketch of Spalding from *Mind Magazine*.
3. Manuscripts and papers by Spalding.
4. David Bruton's eulogy of Spalding.
5. Dr. Neva Dell Hunter's recollections of Spalding, as recounted by Lois Binford Proctor.
6. A miscellany of letters, photographs, and other Spalding memorabilia.

Every effort has been made to ensure that the materials reproduced in the third section (mss and papers) are Spalding's own compositions. Quotation marks have been used to signal titles improvised where none appeared in the original.

With Volume 6, the Spalding "canon" can be presumed closed, with confidence that its message, of benefit to millions over some three-quarters of a century, has been presented in the fullness of its content and human interest.

ARTHUR VERGARA
Editor

PAGES FROM
MIND MAGAZINE
1935 - 1937

THE MESSAGE AND THE MESSENGER

EDITOR'S NOTE:* Ever since Volume I, *Life and Teaching of the Masters of the Far East*, by Baird T. Spalding, appeared, and continuing through the present Volume III, the articles appearing in *Mind Magazine* and the *India Tour Lessons* [Vol. IV], there has been a vast amount of speculation on the part of various students of truth throughout the world. This speculation has varied from one extreme to another, but this speculation is the result of looking at the whole situation from a purely external point of view.

It is time that the mass of humanity learn to distinguish between the message and the messenger; the Truth and the vehicle through which Truth is presented to the world. Truth is the same regardless of the book that presents it or the teacher who proclaims it. It is not the setting through which Truth is presented that should be the point of consideration but the amount of Truth that is given. Learning to distinguish between the thing that is taught and the manner in which it is taught comprises all the difference between confusion and illumination.

There is nothing taught in the *Life and Teaching of the Masters of the Far East* that is not contained in

*[Feb. 1936]

the most ancient religious writings of Hindu philosophy. Nor is there anything that is taught in these writings that is not taught or implied in modern religion or metaphysics. There is nothing in Mr. Spalding's writings that is not duplicated in the Bible or the practices of Jesus Christ. The setting, the story may have shades of difference, but the truth presented is identically the same if one has the discernment to read them aright. The authority of any individual who dares to declare the truth as it is revealed to him is always challenged. The people of two thousand years ago challenged the authority of Christ. They proclaimed Him a heretic and crucified Him for blasphemy. They tormented and humiliated Him for teaching the very things for which we now worship Him. Time has enabled us to separate His mission and His message from the incidents surrounding Him and His works from the environment in which they were performed, of which we have now lost sight. Now, we must lose sight of incident and environment in which present man labors to give the same Truth to the world and look to the Truth that has lived and does live eternally.

In our everyday life we are inclined to say that "distance lends enchantment." We are slow to take into account that this fact largely influences us in our estimates of incidents and people in our practical everyday activities. What might happen in India might have the reverse reaction for an American that it has for a Hindu and vice versa. The people of India would consider the activities of certain people in America as the unmistakable signs of a Master. Our Bible might be considered as presumptuous and startling to those who look to the Bhagavad Gita or the Vedas as the sacred books whose pages contain for them the essence of Truth. A Hindu might well come to America to witness the modern miracles accredited to certain people of this country, and we would consider it a mark of their intelligence should they do so. But should we journey to India to witness the same performances and to receive the same teaching, it would be considered by some other Americans as an indication of mental weakness. But is it a case of mental weakness in either event, or does it not indicate the thirst for true knowledge that burns alike in the common heart of mankind? The fact is, whether it be the teaching of Hindu, Christ, or modern metaphysician, the purport of any true message is that the Truth is to be found in the human heart and the contact is made right where we may find ourselves at any moment of our existence.

If there is that in the teachings of any individual, in the Bible or any other one of the sixty sacred books of the world that will give us light on our own divinity, let us consider it. If it points out the Infinite Principle of life, whether we call that principle by the name of God, Brahm, Rah or Ain Soph, let us drink from its fountain of life. If we will get away from the setting in which the Truth is presented and look for Truth at its Source, we will find it.

Religious prejudice is the most deeply seated prejudice in human nature. If we would find Truth, we must rise above our own weaknesses and dare to face the Truth wherever it may be found and whatever its discovery may do to the narrow confines of our own beliefs and speculations.

To quote Mr. Spalding in one of his forthcoming lessons: "The Masters look to America as containing one hundred and twenty million Masters." That is their way of declaring all men as Masters. To contact your Master is to find your Divine Self. Whatever presentation of Truth helps you to attain this end is vital. If you lose sight of this point, all teaching so far as you are concerned is vain.

Whether it be a Master, a Saint, a Guru—to the Hindu it means one who is the mouthpiece of the Infinite. In America, whether it be a priest, a rector, a preacher, the title is supposed to indicate the same mission. Whether we are true to the trust which we have assumed is a matter for each individual to fathom for himself. For the rest of us, our mission is to discern the Truth which emanates, whether it be of God or whether it be the fabrications of our own system of mental delusions.

BIOGRAPHICAL SKETCH:
BAIRD T. SPALDING

THE SPALDING family originated in England and it was there that Baird T. Spalding was born. At the age of four he went to India, and India has been his home ever since, although his education and work have taken him to all parts of the world.

Soon after his arrival in India, Baird enrolled in the preparatory school for the University. At the age of seventeen he finished at the University. After two years in California he went to Germany, where he studied for eight years at Heidelberg, returning to California for post-graduate work in Archaeology at Berkeley and Stanford.

Baird T. Spalding comes from a family that has lived and worked for over three hundred years in India and the Gobi desert. It was through a discovery of his great-grandfather that the Spalding Foundation had its inception, leading to the discovery of the ruins in the Gobi where the Foundation is working today.*

This is the story. Baird Spalding's great-grandfather was engaged in trade and was taking a load of goods down the Ganges. It was at the flood season, but being unaccustomed to the conditions, the party kept on until the waters were sweeping away the banks. The

*[1935]

17

boats were pulled out on a shelf. One boat was along-side of a wall that had been exposed. A native broke through the wall and out of it fell several gold pieces. Inside was a vault, and in this vault was a book of gold. This book was the second of a series and in it was given the location of the other books. The books give a concise history of the old civilization, designating longitudes and latitudes. The second to the last page of each book is a map of the location of the other books. The last page is a map of the location of the cities. It was realized that if these people knew how to work longitudes and latitudes by finding their point of departure, it would be possible to find the locations of the cities. The engineers working under the Spald-ing Foundation were nineteen years finding the loca-tion of the city in the Gobi, but they struck the ruins when they sank their first shaft.

Spalding's great-grandfather was never in the Gobi. His grandfather went there in 1868, and Baird T. Spalding made his first trip in 1879.*

Today it has been proved conclusively that the so-called legends of the older civilizations are truth. It is known that these older civilizations existed and that the people accomplished more than we have accom-plished today. We know that the greatest civilization known was in this country, right where we are, and in different portions of the North and South American continents, in a continent now submerged in the Pa-cific, and possibly in a continent now submerged in

*Spalding was born May 26, 1857 — *Ed*.

the Atlantic. There is no question but what that great race lived in the spiritual side of life.

Mr. Spalding is in the United States today. His book *Life and Teaching of the Masters of the Far East*, Volume III, is off the press, and Mr. Spalding has been lecturing and answering questions concerning his work in the Gobi and his life with the Masters of the Far East. He plans to visit twenty-five of the principal cities of the United States before departing for India and the Gobi on September 30th.* A growing number of students, authors and scientists are planning to accompany him as far as India, where he will conduct them along the Great Indian Highway to the villages, temples and homes of the Masters of the Far East.

Mind Magazine is now reporting the Spalding lectures and question forums and will feature the questions and answers in its pages each month, together with articles recording the happenings on the world tour.

*Departure was on October 4th, after a month's coast-to-coast promotional tour — *Ed*.

TALK GIVEN AT TRIUNITY, LOS ANGELES, JULY 28, 1935

OUR WORK has been archaeological research and I am not a lecturer. I am an engineer, and our work has been in a field about which we talk little. But because of the inquiries as to whether or not these things are fact and if these people really lived it is necessary to come out and tell some of the results of our contact with the people who lived and who are now living this so-called remarkable life.

To them it is not remarkable. It is the natural sequence of a life well lived. Our research work has proved conclusively that every one of its demonstrations can be proved and that there is a scientific fact back of it. In fact we know today that each accomplishment of any description is brought about by a scientific fact underlying it. A person does not need to wonder or speculate on these conditions. We can use them by stepping forth and becoming one with them. It becomes perfectly simple. The Western world seems to be working through complicated conditions whereas the Eastern world works with them. You cannot accomplish a thing unless you stand one with it. It is not leading from one thing to another but accomplishing one thing and then taking up another thing in a perfectly orderly sequence.

Our research has been carried on so that we can

say, and it will be proved, that there is no such thing as death. It is only the accomplishment of the individual and the mass of individuality. It is accomplished in exactly the same way as we accomplish anything else. It is far easier to accomplish life than death because life is a more magnificent thing. Death occurs when the vibrations become so low that life is crowded out. There is no doubt that the scientific facts will be brought out so that they are explainable.

We will be able to show you a mathematical formula for bodily perfection. It will be presented as simply as the multiplication table. It is being worked out right here in this country now. People look on that as a mystery. It is not. These things can be proved. If we do not believe them we do not have them. If we do not come forth and accept them they are not for us. This research work has been carried on because of our feeling that people would use them at some time.

An older people in an old civilization lived in a higher attitude than we do today. The records they left are most valuable to the civilization of today. If humanity can be assisted by them, so much the better. If they are not practical, we do not want anything to do with them. Consequently, we have tried to bring it down to an actual, practical working basis with no mystery or myth. If that can be taken out, it can be lived and accomplished in every attitude of life. If one person accomplished it, all can and will.

QUESTIONS AND ANSWERS

Q. In Volume III, *Life and Teaching of the Masters of the Far East*, you speak of being with the Masters and arriving at places where it would seem you in the physical could not go. Would you give us a little light on that?

A. Many times the transference of our bodies was without our knowledge. It is evident that if we project our vision to a definite place, we would be at that place the instant the projection is completed. The only thing that keeps us from being at that destination is that we accept that some outer force holds us where we are. If we would let go of that limitation, we would be in the place we vision instantly. We would be in perfect harmony with the condition that would take us instantly to the place where our vision is located. The vibration of the body transferred is much higher. It becomes one with those vibrations which operate at a greater frequency. We have an electronic body which is with us always, and that body is the body in which we actually live. It is only another determination for the actual life we live. As a matter of fact, we have one body in which we live that has all the attributes of being. If we do not make a division, we could be wherever we willed instantly. It is possible to leave behind this body. But it is the greater thing to take it with you always.

Q. Could we bring Emil or any of the other Masters here?

A. I have never attempted it. I stand this way: I am here. If I need them they will be here. Or if they wish to come they are free to come. If we become completely at one with them, we are with them always. The Christ stands where we stand. There is no division except that which man makes.

Q. You said that there was but one presentation of the Christ.

A. There is but one universal Christ of all mankind. If we stand one with Christ, we are that very thing. Jesus presented the Christ to the world, which all men may present if they will.

Q. Is the Christ always a man?

A. The Christ dwells within the individual always.

Q. Wasn't it vibrations that broke down the walls of Jericho?

A. Possibly, but recent excavations show that the walls were undermined. That may have been done by vibrations.

Q. Where is St. Germain?

A. We do not know. We do not know of any location in which he confines himself. All of these people of that high attitude work for the whole world.

St. Germain has chosen to work with many political divisions, but he does not confine himself.

Q. Does every soul have to make the ascension as did Jesus?

A. No. But they will make the ascension as they see it. You are never bound to any one condition or any form of condition. You are bound to your own determination of that condition. You are perfectly free to make the ascension at any instant, and you are always living to a higher level because you are presenting that ideal.

Q. What about those who are supposed to have died?

A. They are not in death. That body is what we look on as inactive. The life is not with that body. It has left that body and goes on just the same. It is only a change, and the death is a mistaken idea.

[UNTITLED]

IT HAS been suggested that I go a little more into detail about the inception of our work. It seems that many do not understand the motive back of starting the work. The work was originated by my great-grandfather, and he organized the foundation under which we are working. It was his purpose to prove whether or not the so-called myths of India had a real foundation in fact and if the reputation of the older civilizations was truth.

It has been claimed in India for centuries that a greater civilization existed. When my great-grandfather started this work it was thought that it would take only about twenty or twenty-five years before they could reach their conclusions. The time passed and only the surface had been touched. In fact, the work in the Gobi alone has been going on for sixty-seven years, and the research work which led up to it was started much earlier than that. The things we found in the Gobi led on and on and brought us right back to this country, the country we had always thought of as a new country. We suddenly found that the greatest race with the highest conceptions had lived in this very country. . . .

We know today that those conclusions are correct. In the last few years we have been led to other conclusions. We find that there have been at least four great

25

civilizations, and it is quite conclusive that evidence will be produced of two more civilizations and that we are now in the sixth civilization that has gone to a high conception and that this civilization will blend into the seventh without going back, as others have done. We are able to show today that a portion of the higher civilization never went back into ignorance and darkness. We are in hopes that we can soon present this as fact. We find many people working along these same lines today and, of course, many minds working tend to bring about results quickly.

We find the seventh race coming on rapidly and close upon us. We believe we shall step forward right into it. It is a stepping up of the process of evolution. Humanity is receiving a greater impetus toward that civilization than would have been possible if those former civilizations had not existed. People are working back to those former accomplishments. It is not necessary to undergo the conditions of today. No human being can make an accomplishment without bringing the whole of civilization a step nearer its goal by that accomplishment. We are so close to that goal today that we do not hesitate to make these statements. Many of them may seem visionary, but I believe nearly everyone today can look forward to seeing the vision an established fact. It is seldom today that you hear anyone saying that a thing is impossible, whereas only a few years ago you heard it on every hand. There has been so much come forth in the last fifteen years that people are really thinking, and that thoughtful attitude alone is of the greatest assistance to humanity.

Definite thought along the right lines helps humanity more than we realize. We never know at what moment the thoughts we send out will bring our neighbor to a greater understanding. Quite often that understanding goes farther than the understanding of the one who sent out the thought, because the recipient thinks more deeply. Through that we find many accomplishments that would not have been brought out for a long time had not someone presented a vision for another to amplify and carry on to a greater determination. The person who put forth the thought may not remember it, but the person who took it may have brought certain methods to bear which showed him that back of that thought was a truth.

We do not know just what our words and thoughts will do if we put them out in the right direction. I think nearly everyone sees that if we send out our thoughts definitely and with the right attitude or perception, when they return they are of vast benefit. That attitude is bringing people to a greater understanding of what vibrations or thought can accomplish. Our scientists are telling us today that we live in vibration, and that everything surrounding us is vibration. Even the hardest steel vibrates and coalesces and is held in that position because of that very vibratory frequency. We know today that our bodies are being held together by that very same thing. It will be determined that it is spiritual.

Scientists are saying that all things can be reduced to vibration at least. Many persons are going beyond that and asking, "What is the real thing?" Others say, "What can you determine it but God?" That is a great forward step. I remember one of my own professors who was making deductions and pointing out the conditions that could be brought about through them. He carried them back until he said, "What is the ultimate? My determination is God!" That happened years ago. Many today are following along that same line, bringing everything down to a spiritual determination.

Of course, for many years, we have looked on that as something that could not be classified. But how can we classify a thing unless we first classify it through thought? That attitude of thought brings that determination into existence because of the impetus given it by the thought back of it. It is getting rid of the hard and fast rule that unless we can see, touch and feel a thing, it does not exist. There is scarcely a scientist today who does not accept that back of everything is a determining element that brings it into existence and that when in existence, the very power that brought it into existence actuates it in every dimension.

Many people doubt the existence of life after the so-called experience of death. That experience is no more than the receding of the body vibrations to the point where the life element is crowded out. Since that element vibrates at a certain determined rate, it can not associate itself with that body. Evidently it goes on seeking a higher determination with which it can associate. We fully believe that our research will go on to a point where we can prove that the life element begins to assemble a new body the moment it leaves the old body.

These things have come to a point where they are

not looked on as mythical or superstitious. People are accepting them as actual fact. There is definite scientific fact back of them. If a fact is accomplished, there is a definite scientific determination back of it. Everything is accomplished under a definite law. Every individual works with that law if they accomplish anything, even to walking or breathing. There is no doubt about that. There are many manifestations which we are unable to determine yet, but there are many people working along these lines and in a very short time remarkable results will be brought forth. Every thought, instantly it is put forth, reverts back to the principle or law. At that time that thought becomes a very determining factor, always. It is not a hit-or-miss condition but a complete understanding of every condition.

You are going to see that nearly everyone will be working in that very attitude of thought. It is far better to work in that one-pointed attitude than it is to scatter your thoughts and thus scatter your forces over a great many fields at once. We should have some great condition which we can determine and through that determination accomplish. We have been going around in circles long enough. We must accomplish one thing and then go on to the next in a definite progression. That is the attitude of a large portion of the Eastern and Western world today. That is where the East and the West are going to meet. Each has a great deal for the other.

The evolving of the physical body of the Western people has not come about in a hit-or-miss manner. There has been a very determining factor back of it. People can always bring out a greater attitude of thought with better bodies and better surroundings. In evolving the physical body there have been many sidetracks and many things we look on as outside the spiritual, but that does not make any difference. If we have our eyes fixed on the goal we shall accomplish it, accomplishing through a spiritual fact with the determination to go ahead and accomplish in that very attitude, seeing no other.

That certainly is what the world is looking forward to today. We may be unconscious of it, but it was the same when our forefathers were using the tallow candle. The electric light was there all the time. It only took a man with vision who could see that if he brought into existence a small enough filament, by passing a current through it the filament would become hot enough to give off light. It was the same with the radio and many other inventions. But we are going on with a greater impetus because we have accepted those things. It is not necessary that we understand these things. But when we do become conscious of them, we have even greater things presented to us. Thus we go on, step by step, until we see that there is no turning back, nor do we wish to turn back.

QUESTIONS AND ANSWERS

Q. Do the books of gold spoken of in your biographical sketch have the same texts?

A. They treat of the same civilization, but each book has a different text. These books were not written at the time of this civilization. The conditions were such that it was thought that many of the records of this former civilization were being neglected and that the records would be lost in the years to come. The books were written to point to definite locations where the records would be found. The books are more or less glossaries, written so that they would stimulate research to the point where the records would be brought out.

Q. Were all the books found in India?

A. All five of the books are in India. The four we found were there, and the fifth is there. We have found ruins of cities in Alaska also, but little else. Near the spot where the McKenzie River empties into the ocean we have sunk shafts and found ruins of cities. The carvings on the building blocks show that the people of this civilization knew the art of carving as did the people whose civilization we are unearthing in the Gobi. We have not been able to carry on the research work in Alaska to the point where we have their records, but we have

31

found records in the Gobi which refer to points where the records were placed. It took us twelve years in the Gobi after we had sunk the first shaft before we opened the first vault. After that, it took us a little more than four years to open three more. They are in a fine state of preservation.

Q. Will you comment on the appearance and disappearance of the Masters and their assistance to you in your work?

A. We saw that happen many times. While we do not know the modus operandi of that appearance and disappearance, we do not look on it as mysterious, although we did at first. It was one of the outstanding experiences of our three and one-half years with those people. It is difficult to elaborate on it as we do not understand it ourselves. Many times when we were away from our source of supply we sat down and prepared to eat and food appeared for us. But we came to a point where we knew that we should not depend on these people. They have told us many times of the locations of the ruins and records of the older civilizations. Had we depended wholly on their information, we would have learned nothing of the method by which the ruins and records could be found; so we chose to go on with our surveys. We have proved that we can reach the same determinations by surveys. Today we are depending more on what these people teach us, and we are going on with the work much more rapidly. But with all of that, we do not depend on them for our supplies. We take our supplies in with us and keep them ahead as much as possible. We have no fear of running out, since we have been supplied so often. All of our water is carried 350 miles by camels. It is the remoteness of the place that has kept it free from vandalism.

It is difficult to explain these people other than to tell of the remarkable things they accomplish. When the necessity for the accomplishment arises, they step forth and accomplish. We have come to rivers and seen them step forth and walk across on the water. They do not look on that as miraculous. It is accomplished by a definite principle. It is done instantly and without a word being spoken. We have pictures of six men walking on the water and of a seventh man stepping forth onto it.

Q. Were you with Emil and Jast when they went through the burning forest?

A. I was. That is the only outstanding experience of which we have no photographs. There were only the three of us. Had I had a camera with me I would have forgotten it. When I stepped forth between those two men, a great archway opened through the fire. To me it was the last straw. That was in 1895.

Q. Will you tell us of the Healing Temple?

A. It is an open temple with eight arches terminating in a great dome. We have never seen anyone officiating in that temple, nor have we ever heard a word said about healing. But everyone who even walks through the temple evidently is benefited. We can not say that everyone is healed, but we know of many healings accomplished there. In five instances we have kept the people with us. One man was carried into the temple on a stretcher in the last stages of ossification. He could not move. In forty-five minutes he arose from the stretcher and walked out of the temple completely out of the condition of ossification. Afterwards he worked with our party. There was the case of the four-year-old Mohammedan child. I held the child in my two hands and there seemed to be no weight to his body. In less than twenty minutes the child got out of the mother's arms and ran out of the temple. The mother could hardly believe he was her child. The form and flesh filled out right before our eyes. We have photographs taken both before and after the healing.

Q. Will you tell us about trying to sing, "Hail, Hail, the Gang's All Here," when you were in the temple?

A. We were told that an inharmonious sound could not be uttered in the temple. We tried to sing, "Hail, Hail, the Gang's All Here," and no sound came forth. We then just said, "Hail, Hail, Hail," and the words rang out as though amplified a thousand times.

Q. How much would it cost to go to the temple?

A. Your expense would have to include going to Calcutta. From there you would make the eight-hundred-mile trip to the temple. That would require that you walk at least two hundred and fifty miles. The people who go on those pilgrimages take their time. They live on the country. It takes them a year and four or five months, generally. In the next few years it may be more accessible by airplanes.

[UNTITLED]

I HAVE been asked to explain or amplify my statements regarding the Healing Temple and the connection of the Masters with it.

It is in this temple that the Masters congregate from time to time for meditation and to give instruction. It was on our pilgrimage there that we had the experience of watching twelve and later fifty-two of the party walk calmly and conveniently across the surface of a stream two thousand feet wide, running full bank with a strong current. The remainder of the party spent four days detouring to the nearest bridge and joining those who had crossed on the water in a few minutes.

We had been told that we could accomplish the crossing as had the others, but none of us felt competent enough to make the attempt. We could not grasp the meaning of what we witnessed or understand that it was accomplished by a definite law open to all to use. On the remainder of our journey to the temple, our thoughts were given over to a contemplation of what we had seen and experienced in the short time we had been with the Masters, and in attempting to accept the teaching that what we had seen accomplished we, ourselves, could accomplish in the same way.

From the point of gathering to the temple itself was a distance of two hundred and fifty miles. There were

36

over three hundred of us. Outside of our immediate group, most of the pilgrims were going in search of healing. Emil was in complete charge, and Jast and Neprow made complete arrangements for our group.

It was explained to us that the temple represents the Christ in the individual, and that it is open at all times to everyone for the purpose of healing. It represents the ideal. It was explained further that though the Masters could have healed the pilgrims and thus saved them the journey to the temple, it is their custom to encourage the people to go to the temple with them and learn for themselves that within them is the power that is within the Masters—that they are the same.

We were told that the perfectly harmonious vibrations given out by the temple as the result of its continued use allow nothing of an inharmonious nature to become a part of it. This, we learned, is exactly what takes place in man when he sends forth only harmonious words. We were told that the definite thought condition has been presented so long and definitely in that temple that the whole structure has taken it on, and that unless the thought you attempt to give out is equal to the vibrations of the temple, it cannot be brought forth into words. If your body is responding to a high influence, a lower vibration may impinge, but it is immediately thrown back. Evidently that condition exists in that temple. We learned that the temple has gone on under those conditions for at least eight hundred years. We fully believe that you could build that vibration right into your body where you are today, if you would.

The number and completeness of the healings was

a source of wonder to us. There was no form of service or official ceremony in the temple. We learned that the influence of the vibrations brought about the benefits derived. We saw the instant healing of a child's withered body. We saw fingers restored to a hand. The blind, the deaf and the diseased we saw healed instantly and completely. Everyone who entered the temple went away improved. It was our privilege to keep in contact with some of those who were healed, and in every case the healing was permanent.

The work of the Masters in connection with the temple and all other healing work is done in such a way as to form the ideal in the minds of those healed, teaching them that they, themselves, must do the work instead of looking to any personality to do it for them.

QUESTIONS AND ANSWERS

Q. Is Tibet the only place where these temples exist?

A. We know of their existence in India and Oriental countries. In all probability they are in this country, although we do not know of any definite locations. That does not mean that they do not exist. There are many things we have not seen.

Q. Where are the homes and monasteries of these Masters?

A. Their homes are in India mostly; also in Tibet, China and Persia. They have no monasteries. They have no organization. They say it is the brotherhood of man, and they work independently.

Q. How will we be able to contact these Masters and work with these laws? If we cannot demonstrate them, we feel helpless.

A. We must take the attitude that we know these things exist, and then work with them. These Masters work with everyone. If we accept the conditions, we bring them forth and do live one with them. No one can give you the things they have. They can only show you the way. We must accomplish from within, because everything is within ourselves. Bringing it forth requires that we accept that it is there, that it is completed and for us.

39

That determination brings it into existence and brings us to the point where we project it ourselves. If we depend upon a personality, we build an idol of that personality and lose sight of the ideal it presents.

Q. Are your books actual experience or inspiration?

A. Those books contain the experiences we had with those people for three and one-half years. Everything recorded actually happened, and it happened in the physical. Those people function wholly in spiritual conditions, but they are actually the same as our physical conditions. We have our original notes, and the experiences related in the books were taken wholly from these notes. We were invited to bring with us whom we pleased. We chose the most skeptical, scientific people. We have the reports of all, and all concur in our conclusions. All state that they went doubting and came away fully believing in the existence of these great conditions. I do not blame you for not believing. We did not believe these things would be universally believed. We believe that each individual should inquire. It was necessary for us to bring these things to a point where we could believe them ourselves. I had many experiences with these things before I went on the expedition. I went doubting, but it was less than three weeks after the outset of the expedition that my doubts were cleared.

Q. How is it possible to bring about a great change

under our present conditions in which people are drinking, gambling, smoking and doing everything that is bad?

A. The very expressions you have used allow those conditions to go on today. We use such thoughtless words that we allow those conditions to continue. It is better to say that nothing but good and perfect can be. See absolute perfection for all.

Q. Do you mean that facts are changed by words and thoughts?

A. It is not what the other fellow thinks, it is what we think that brings about conditions. Our thoughts are creative of the very condition. Any person can return those thoughts with such dynamic force that they would destroy the person sending out the thoughts. Are we, then, not responsible?

Q. Can the Masters be contacted at any time?

A. Yes. They are not apart from anyone, and they do not seek seclusion any more than is necessary. They do not localize themselves. All is Spirit. They work in that attitude, and in that attitude they are at any point at any time. How could they not be, if all is Spirit and they work in Spirit? It is the separation *we* make, not the separation *they* make.

Q. Is it possible for these Masters to operate in more than one body at the same time?

A. We know of many instances where these people manifest in three bodies at one time, and of one

41

instance where a man manifests in four bodies.

Q. Are there not Masters of the inner esoteric world prohibited from appearing before the people?

A. We have never known of such a case. There are many who choose to work in silence, but I do not think the choice is made for them.

Q. You were just speaking of how you know of people functioning in different bodies. Would it be possible for Jesus to be functioning in some other body?

A. Why would it necessarily be Jesus? The same Spirit is in all of us.

USE YOUR GOD-GIVEN POWER

I WANT to make clear the fact that I do not claim anything for myself in my books. They are, as the titles imply, the teaching that was given us. Our work has been that of scientific research, and in it we have been helped by the Masters. They have made it possible for us to carry on where otherwise we would have felt powerless. Undoubtedly we gained a great deal spiritually through the contacts with the Masters, yet that contact is open to all. None is turned away. The contact may be made right where you are as well as in India or any other place and comes according to the individual consciousness through the life the individual leads.

Do not disturb yourself concerning the astral plane. Use your God-given power. Elevate your thought to the God thought. Whatever may be your problem, you can find God in it. A Master or teacher can assist you, but he cannot live your life. Go to him for inspiration. Call upon God when you want to know the Truth.

You know that it is God you are seeking. Do not go through the personality of Jesus. Go through the Christ in you. The Christ in you is God. By contacting God in you, you will attain. Jesus tried to show that as the source of His power.

There is no advantage in praying to an individual

God. See God as a great Power, and demand of that Power. Prayer raises your vibration to the point where you can contact the power of the universal consciousness. When you get the eternal life thought in your consciousness, you can attain to any degree of spirituality. No one can give you the rules to go by. You must work out the formula for yourself.

Moses worked to bring out the Babylonian records. In the originals of his work he gave reference to the original records which he found and copied. He failed to complete the work, and when the translators tried to complete it, they failed. Whereas his work attempted to give the idea of universal life, it has been handed down as a set of laws.

Today large numbers of people are rediscovering that God has always lived in man. They are outgrowing the orthodox teachings based on self-interest. Through their new understanding they will erase every limitation.

QUESTIONS AND ANSWERS

Q. What preparation is necessary before we can contact the Masters?

A. We are not conscious of any definite form of preparation. Our contact has been of long standing, but we know of people who have contacted them without any outer preparation. We do not know what their attitude of thought was, but in all probability it is the desire or mental attitude which brings one into contact with them. We have not made a study of these conditions because to us the contact seems a perfectly natural one. It is often said that if we are prepared for a Master to appear, he will appear. It is not necessary to go to India or any other place. The attitude is within, and the moment we are ready, the way is open.

Q. Do we meet these Masters in the flesh as we meet each other here today?

A. Yes, just as definitely as that. We can photograph them with the same process we use for photographing in everyday life.

Q. Does that include Jesus?

A. Yes. We know and we do not hesitate to say that Jesus is living in the same body that was crucified. We do not see any great difference in the Masters and ourselves physically. There is a finer look about them than about most people, but there is nothing definite to distinguish them.

Q. Should we objectify our desires or put them forth in definite form, knowing that they are already in existence? Should we say that we want a thing or should we say, "God's will be done"?

A. If we say, "God's will be done," that is the highest attitude. If we say that a thing is ours, that puts us in an attitude of thought of accepting that it is ours. You could not think of a thing unless it was already in existence for you. Every expression can be carried out with that thought in view. Take the attitude that you are one with it and that it is yours to bring forth.

Q. If Jesus manifests in the flesh, is that not discouraging to those who have buried the bodies of their loved ones?

A. It would be the greatest encouragement, would it not? He has gone through all those experiences and come out of what we call death completely. Even though your friends have passed on, they have not died. There is no death. Your loved ones are all in existence, only you are unconscious of them.

Q. How can we avoid the working of the law of Karma?

A. The moment we let go of it, we do not have it. If we misuse a law, we can turn and use it more completely than we could ever misuse it. If we would accomplish all things in this life, we would never need to reincarnate. It is only that we accept Karma that we work through it. Many think it is necessary to come back through reincarnation. Suppose you say that two and two is three. Really it is four. You did nothing to distort Principle by saying that it is three. If you want to get rid of the mistake, you erase three and put four in its place. The attitude that we are building up Karma is that attitude that we are distorting Principle. But we have not harmed Principle.

Q. Is it necessary to overcome all flesh?

A. It is necessary not to overcome all flesh, but to put a better conception upon it by the resurrection of this body from a material to a spiritual condition. If we come into true spirit, this flesh is immortalized always. Why overcome flesh? It is perfectly beautiful and pure if we overcome the idea that has held it out of that condition.

TALK GIVEN IN HOLLYWOOD,
AUGUST 14, 1935

IT HAS been suggested that something might be said about the I AM and its relation to the individual, and the individual's responsibility in connection with the I AM.

A true determintion of the I AM is the Christ in the individual. There may be many divisions of that, but those divisions are the determining factors that man gives to them. The true I AM is the Christ in the individual always standing forth and manifesting divinity. That is where man belongs. That is his high dominion. That is where man always has been and always will be. Man could not get out of that attitude if he tried.

Many persons may think that is a very bold statement. Here is the scientific truth back of it. Were this statement not a fact, there would not be a human body in existence today. We are all manifesting it at a certain rate of vibration. We can bring that vibration down or keep it in its dominion. Man can never take himself out of that attitude. Every scientist is accepting that if man got out of his true vibration for one instant, his body would fly to pieces.

There are, of course, many determining factors which man can accept for himself, but it is his own attitude of thought. Your attitude of thought is only the determining factor of that projection which you have found. That does not make any difference to the I AM or the Christ. You can lower the vibration of the body by that projection. We can see the result of the lowering of the vibrations of the body. If we all stand where we belong, nothing but harmony can exist. We are like the small child who was sent to the music master for his first lesson and who insisted that he should learn inharmony before he learned harmony. We are all children trying to learn inharmony.

Always, man's divinity is man's higher attitude. It can be proved in every instance. We can show it photographically. We can show that if you are standing forth with that dominion, your body stands forth on the plate in a blaze of light. We can show you the light emanating from the body. If you will go on with that determination, you can see after four or five seconds just the dim outline of the body on the film.

Now you cannot photograph anything of a psychic determination. You can only photograph true emanations. This proves conclusively that the I AM exists. If it did not exist, you could not get a photograph of it.

If a higher attitude were not in existence, you could not think of it. There is no question but that this condition will be proved. I said recently that a mathematical formula, as simple as the multiplication table, would be presented to you soon, which would give you a formula for bodily perfection. There is no scientific discovery made which has not already been in existence and used at some former time. The vibrations are there, and it is natural to pick them up and bring them into use. These may go on to higher and greater things than the older civilizations experienced. This civilization is going on to a greater attainment than any other civilization. We know that in this very country there existed a civilization which went on to a greater determination than we have today. We are just beginning to image what they accomplished. We are going to accomplish even greater. That is what was meant when Jesus said, "The works that I do shall he do also; and greater works than these shall he do." That was thought to be supernatural, and it has taken on a mysterious appearance, but it is a perfectly natural condition. Science is coming to prove all these things. Science is coming to see that there is no "phenomenon" in nature. Science will tell you today that we shall take everything we need right from the atmosphere. It will not be a great while until we are accelerating the slow process of nature.

When Jesus multiplied the loaves and the fishes, it was pronounced supernatural. That was what man named it. If man today would stand forth and name himself the Christ, what could happen but that the Christ would come forth? These things can be taken out of the mysterious into the open light of day. These things will be accomplished right here in this country, and you are going to see them accomplished. We are not talking of future things. They are here now. *It is only our attitude which keeps them away from us now.* See how long we have kept modern inventions away. The things we pronounced as fakes fifteen years ago we accept today, and we live wholly unconscious of them. It is the recognition of the method by which a thing is brought into existence that gives it its value. When our forefathers went about with candles to light their way, electricity was already here. Man had only to see that if he made a filament and put an electrical current through it, he would have an electric light. We are wholly unconscious today of the very method whereby electricity is being used. We see the radio and many other inventions in use. We are just now on the threshold of many wonderful things. Why do we hesitate to take the step and declare that we are one with these things?

That manifestation, if we hold it forth, we must become.

QUESTIONS AND ANSWERS

Q. What power do we contact beyond our own Christ consciousness?

A. There is no other power beyond our own. Man stands forth one with power. The moment he contacts it he is one with it. It is not God's fault, and it makes no difference to power if man makes no contact with it. It is your own determination. If we recognize it as something beyond ourselves, we are degenerating. If we do not see the thing and rise to the condition, we keep ourselves away from it. It lies right within and no other place.

Q. You maintain that all the power in the universe is within ourselves?

A. The very starting point is right within you. It has always been there or we would never have presented the ideal. You cannot imagine a thing unless you can accomplish it. It is necessary for the human being to come into existence to show the manifestation of God power, and that is the only medium through which the God power can come into existence. If we lower ourselves below that attitude, it is our own determination. You present the Christ every moment you present a high attitude.

Q. Even if you declare yourself anti-Christ could you still demonstrate great wealth?

A. Man does present the Christ every time he accomplishes. It does not matter what he thinks about it. It does not matter how man accomplishes. Through the accomplishment he is going to be brought to the acceptance of the truth. Man may do un-Christlike things, but he is still the Christ. He only thinks himself out of the Christ attitude and thereby accomplishes selfish things, but he pays for them.

Q. Isn't it being demonstrated that plant life is capable of experiencing pain?

A. Yes. But man must impose that condition upon the plant. It is the conditions that man imposes upon himself that cause his pain. But if that portion of the brain which causes man to impose such conditions were entirely blanked, man would never think of inflicting pain on any man, plant or animal.

Q. Does it make any difference in what manner or method a person worships God? Can he shake off the Omnipotent within him?

A. No.

Q. Can immortality be proved physically?

A. Yes, physically and mentally. We can show you photographs of immortality after the physician has pronounced a man dead. We observe the natural body while the camera observes the emanation. It has intelligence and will power. Life, after what we pronounce death, does go on.

Q. If you have those proofs, you would lift a great burden from the minds of men by making them known.

A. It will take many demonstrations and proofs before the orthodox individual will accept it. It took Marconi many years to bring the radio to the point of determination to put it into practical use. The scientists of the world pronounced the radio a fake at first. Today we are using it in every walk of life. It was the same with X-ray. It was called the devil's own concoction.

Q. Why hasn't the I AM Presence worked?

A. The joker is man. It is up to man to will or not to will. Man is the determining factor. The unsuccessful man is the man who does not raise himself to the point where he *knows*. It does not matter what the other fellow is doing. "I must be about my Father's business." Jesus never lived outside the Father. That Father was the principle. If man would live one with the Father or the principle, he would accomplish greater things than Jesus. "Greater works than these shall he do." Jesus knew that humanity would accomplish greater things.

DIVINE MASTERY

UNTIL RECENT years in the Western world, a man who claimed to be divine was called a heretic. The Eastern attitude is that it is heresy to accept less than Divinity. Now how did the Western world accept the term *heresy* for the claim of man to Divinity? It was only that someone had told us that it was heresy. Instead of thinking for ourselves, we took the word of another. Man has been taught to fear God. It is well known today that if we do not fear an animal, it will not harm us; and if we do not fear a condition, that condition cannot come into our lives. How can we fear the greatest determining influence that belongs to humanity—man's true Divinity? How could we even express fear toward it unless we were taught that fear?

Jesus has told us that what one has accomplished, all can, and this is not only possible but is positive the moment we realize that Principle exists.

We saw a very remarkable demonstration of that positive attitude and what one man could accomplish before a horde of advancing bandits. I have recounted the incident in Volume III of *Life and Teaching of the Masters of the Far East*. It shows the power of one man in his divine mastery to turn the energy of a bandit band to his and his neighbors' protection. The resistance of the bandits to the love presented to them caused the emanations of destruction they were putting forth to return to themselves.

It is that condition that is changing war today and which will do away with it eventually. Today not only thousands but millions are saying "No" to war. Humanity is aware of the fact that another great struggle would mean oblivion, and there are enough people saying that instead of civilization going out, the nation or individual declaring war is going out instead.

QUESTIONS AND ANSWERS

Q. You tell of many teachings from Jesus that are somewhat different from those of the New Testament. Is there a possibility that we will have a new translation?

A. There are people working on the translation of the original that was translated from the Aramaic to the Greek. We are told that it will take another four years. I do not think it will be put out as a new testament. It is now known that two hundred thousand years elapsed between the events of the first chapter of Genesis and the second chapter of Genesis. Again, at the time when Moses was reported to have been found in the bulrushes he would have been ninety years of age. That story was purely allegorical.

Q. How should we convey a constructive thought to someone afflicted?

A. Present God to him as the greatest thought. Then we are presenting a condition that lifts him right out of affliction. If we present God, we correct any condition.

Q. In order to realize the Christ consciousness should we affirm it to ourselves?

57

A. It is necessary to present the Christ, and the Christ is far more than an affirmation because the instant we present the Christ, we must see ourselves as that very thing. The affirmation will bring us to the realization, unless we get mixed up in the affirmation. Jesus said, "I see the Christ in every face and in every form. When the first child was born, the Christ was born." You do not need an affirmation. The trouble is that we take something and make a crutch out of it instead of standing on our own feet.

Q. Is the Lord's Prayer as we have it in our Bible a true translation?

A. It is a true translation of the Jewish translation. But it was not put forth by Jesus.*

Q. What is the difference between Spirit and Soul?

A. There is no difference. You can not make a separation. Spirit, Soul and body are one.

*See p. 141.

[UNTITLED]

JESUS TAUGHT that the Father is the principle by which humanity might accomplish, that Life must live, that there is no mystery in His deeds and teachings.

Principle cannot change. You can overlook it for eternity if you will, but the moment you return to it, you will return to perfect condition. Your body gets the result of that determination. One knowing and using that principle would not hesitate to walk upon the water. You have been told often that if one endeavors to accomplish and succeeds, all can. The power has always existed and always will exist. Why is it kept away? It is because we put up the barriers of disbelief.

The power that brings into existence a mechanical device could instantly bring into existence the condition that device produces. We talk across great distances with the modern telephone. There are many people, however, who talk over great distances without any device whatever. Telepathy is recognized as an established fact. There is a great power contained in mental telepathy. It is God speaking to God. There are many who may say such a statement is sacrilegious; such a statement is just as definite as the statement that we are living today. Humanity is going to see that it is far better to be in positive influences at all times. Then we are going to take the great step forward.

These are not conclusions of our group alone. Numbers of people and groups are working along the same lines. Use of these facts will bring us into complete harmony, complete unity, where man has accomplished and where he belongs.

Now it does not make any difference whether the body of humanity believes these things today. The facts are evident. When Jesus said he had overcome death he spoke truly. Thousands upon thousands today, seeing that truth, will know that this body is immortal, pure, perfect and indestructible. The mystery is gone and we are on the threshold of complete understanding.

QUESTIONS AND ANSWERS

Q. Rosicrucian and theosophic teaching is that the body of Jesus was prepared from birth for 30 years, then it was taken over by a spirit. Jesus withdrew and the Christ spirit used the body for the three years.

A. That is a part of the truth. The truth is this. The body of every woman is prepared for an immaculate birth. Every child is born perfect. It is only the thoughts of the human that lower it. Every child born is a Christ child. The Rosicrucians in the early days taught that. Now they teach the concept of Buddhism, which has been misinterpreted from many translations.

Your churches teach you that Jesus was the Son of God and that we are conceived in sin and born into iniquity. That is false. If we would see every child always as the Christ, we would never have our present-day conditions. Jesus' life was perfectly practical. He did nothing which He claimed to be miraculous, and He did nothing which man can not do. There isn't a thing in the records from which you could even imagine that Jesus presented the idea that He was the only Son of God. There are many false and many true translations of the Bible. Had Jesus declared it for Himself alone, He could never have been the Christ. He simply presented the Christ to the world. He presented the ideal which humanity could follow. He didn't take it upon Himself to correct humanity. Some declare Him the only son of God, but if they would follow in His footsteps, they would become the same. Jesus sent out the vibrations which lifted humanity. No one ever accomplishes anything with a high attitude of thought but that he lifts the whole world. If we lived outside of perfection, our whole bodies would fly to pieces. The position would be so reversed that our bodies would return to the substance from which they came.

Q. Do you think all humanity could raise itself in one incarnation?

A. Yes. This very instant. It is man's rightful inheritance. It is here for us. Had it not been here and already accomplished, we would never have thought of it.

Q. Do you think many are making the accomplishment?

A. Yes, thousands. Fifty years ago people would have said you were crazy to make such statements, but India has been living in this conception for hundreds of years.

Q. If a Master were in this room and there were someone here who was sick, would he be healed?

A. In all probability, yet there might be a Master in this room and if the sick person did not see perfection, he would not be healed. The person seeing perfection is the Master. There can be no sick condition if you present the Christ. Then you are the Master, and you have accomplished perfection. It is the place of every person to present the Divinity to himself.

Q. I have the desire to see and talk to Jesus in the tangible form.

A. Who keeps Him away from you but yourself? Let go of the self who is keeping Him away. All you have to do is to accept that He is right here. Your desire is not correct or you would have accomplished it. If it were correct, you would accomplish it immediately.

Q. Was your contact with Jesus conscious with you?

A. I never sought it. I opened the way for all contact.

[UNTITLED]

NO INFORMED person questions the fact that the truths in the Bible are obscured by mistranslation and interpolation. My statements are not intended to tear down in any way its teachings; they are intended to give a better understanding and show that we have evolved to the need for a greater definition. We are now looking toward the actual light.

You can extract four stories from the Bible — two by reading it forward and two by reading it backward. Why? The Bible was so written as to mystify the old Chaldean priests who were perverting the teachings. For that reason, its teachings became wholly mysterious.

After a recent talk, a gentleman came to me with a translation he had made of the Lord's Prayer. He had taken each word of the original and traced its meaning back to the root words. He has a translation which shows that the attitude of Jesus was not one of supplication. His prayer was significant beyond mere petition. The suggested translation ran:

In this manner therefore you do make your adoration and do turn to your inherent power. Be you reborn by the exercise of this mental power that uplifts you to the homeland above. You do grant us this light of life in order that we may loose ourselves from this harvest of discord only as we dissolve or erase the har-

*vester or sinner who harvests it. Nay, you do draw us
back from the dangers of the conditions of the flesh.*

That is a very literal translation. Going from mouth
to mouth, folklore crept into the Lord's Prayer, and
a sentence here and a sentence there were changed.
The individual today must recapture the original
meaning. We may now step out of a condition which
we believe submerges us.

We need beg for nothing. We turn reverently to the
power within which lifts our thoughts to union with
the creative forces. All power flows to us when we look
to it alone, to the power that we *are*, the power that
God *is*. Thus by conscious unity with God, we cease
to sow tares and begin to build for the future in harmony with His laws.

When humanity is in the depths of its own mistakes,
it must be lifted up. People have been reaping what
they have sown. But letting go of the condition, they
release themselves, which is the only forgiveness. By
forgiving, they are forgiven. God does not grant. Man
must work according to law.

We repeat the word *sin*, and every time we do, we
fasten it not only to ourselves, but upon the whole
human race. It is often said that the child is conceived
in iniquity and born in sin. There is nothing further
from the truth than that. A favorite statement of Jesus
was, "I see the Christ in every face and in every form.
When the first child was born, the Christ was born."

If we let the child alone, we never submerge him.
The influence surrounding him would keep him completely. All we need to do is to see the Christ in that
child. The moment we present that child as the

Christ, we bind ourselves together with that child in the greatest enlightenment. It is well known to science that if one atom of our body were out of place, it would cease to exist. Jesus took no attitude of thought save that of the Christ. He presented to humanity in a straightforward, simple way what it could and must present to itself.

Jesus demonstrated, and gave the definitions of, the Christ. It is that attitude of human form that allows God, or Principle, to flow through the universe. It takes energy to do that, but the energy itself builds itself into this body until we become completely aware of it.

We hear many say that we must go through life after life to accomplish these things. This human form is capable of doing anything you wish. There is no limitation put on it one way or the other. You can be just as unlimited in discord as you wish. But the moment you turn from it, you are out of it. Jesus said, "in the twinkling of an eye." That did not mean that we need go through rebirth after rebirth. When He talked, He talked from experience.

When it is said that this is the thirty-sixth time of His reappearance, it is not meant to imply that it is through reincarnation. He said it was His privilege because of the great enlightenment that had been shown Him. He could work in any sphere and on many planes unknown to us. The human eye does not record them. There are thousands of people who have followed Him and had similar experiences, living in a condition of greater vibratory influence.

There was not just one appearance of a man who

could stand forth as the Christ. Jesus never claimed that He was the only one to portray the Christ. In all probability the one man has come forth thirty-six times in periods of great stress and misunderstanding. Many others have done likewise. Were it not for this fact, humanity could easily have lost contact with the great understanding long ago.

Every attitude of living responds to a certain vibratory influence or frequency. We live on those very planes by the very attitude we take toward those conditions. Therefore we can progress only as our thoughts progress. The ideal we project, we accomplish. We can project an ideal this instant, and in succeeding instants greater and greater ideals. We project along a definite line toward accomplishment. Our trouble is that we project an idea, and because we do not see it instantly, we turn back and stop it from coming into existence. The moment we doubt, we put up a wall. It is a wall that cannot be penetrated until it is dissolved in our thoughts.

Dominion has been given to us, and we can make it an actual fact. It does not require begging for anything. It is a standing forth and becoming one with that very thing.

QUESTIONS AND ANSWERS

Q. Is the changing of vibrations brought about by a mental attitude?

A. We can control every vibration by mental attitude. It is the attitude we take which brings about the change.

Q. Are we conscious of raising the vibrations of the body?

A. We become conscious that it can be accomplished. About the only explanation that I have that is different is this. You could not say the word *God* once and have the vibrations of your body respond to the lower frequency in which it was before you said that word. I am an engineer, not a teacher. We have carried on our research purposely to determine if these things are of any effect. If they can not be brought out and made practical, we do not want anything to do with them. We believe they can.

Q. Was Chander Sen resurrected?

A. Evidently Chander Sen had passed away. One of our party placed his hand on him and said that he was not breathing. Emil appeared and said that Chander Sen had passed away. We were told that it was an easy matter for us to assist him to return and take his body. Jesus and two others appeared and we all gathered around the couch where the body was lying. The body disappeared, and a few days later Chander Sen appeared as a man of about forty years. The words are recorded in the books.

Q. I infer that in the days of that civilization, people lived in the realization of a spiritual life.

A. Yes. They lived in the highest conception of man's identity, and with man accomplishing everything he wished. The Masters of today live in just such a way.

Q. I am glad you are breaking up the idea that we must look to someone else.

A. "Behold God" was the greatest sermon ever preached. With that condition there can be no error. Man must get out of the rut. The Master can only lead the way. When you accomplish Christ, you see that it belongs to you. If you won't claim it, you must always stay outside. If you incorporate it, you can't keep it out.

Q. Then we who have been in the theosophy field have been on the wrong track?

A. Not necessarily. It may have been the means of bringing you to the accomplishment.

Q. Were these teachings in existence before the Israelites?

A. No. It is the teaching of the Israelites.

Q. The Avatar is closer to Principle, but is that the essence of his message?

A. Yes. The path which he shows, or the life he lives, becomes the path for all.

[UNTITLED]

SCIENCE IS fast unfolding the true story of the evolution of this earth. We are learning the story of Lemuria, the continent sunk beneath the waters of the Pacific, as well as the story of Atlantis. We do not say that there was a localized continent known as Atlantis. Evidence is strong that there was a complete band of land around the earth. The people spoke one language. Our language takes many of its words from that old language. The continent was known as Mu and the people as Pan. Atlantis means a universal people who spoke a universal language spoken throughout the earth by one race and one people. They did live as one people and almost as one family.

At the close of the Atlantean period certain individuals were led to places of refuge, and from these survivors was founded the new race.

Those people lived in the spiritual side of life, knowing and seeing nothing of the material side. That was the reason for their great accomplishments. To them all was spiritual. Every accomplishment was made under a scientific fact termed spiritual. There was a complete understanding of all conditions. The early Sanskrit records give us insight into their lives and accomplishments. They lived and thought definitely.

We are just beginning to accomplish what those people lived. Just as we live with the electric light, airplane and radio, those people communicated from

71

one point and kept in constant communication with that point. From the city in the Gobi where our foundation is working they kept in communication with a city the ruins of which are thirty miles from Knoxville, Tennessee.

There was a civilization that worked in art and science far greater than anything we know today. There is a point of that civilization on the British Columbia coast, another in the Mesa Verde, and another in Mexico about one hundred and sixty miles from our border, the ruins of which we have investigated. We believe we shall be able to show that the city in Mexico took its water from the great lake at the head of the Colorado River. The Colorado Gorge is one hundred thousand years old. Those people built aqueducts, beautifully paved. The process of excavation has been slow because of the colossal size of the ruins.

Our object is to bring out all the records and put them at the disposal of the world. With the help of the Masters we have been able to make translations of records, dating far back, of the knowledge of our material world. Our own limitations have kept us from authenticating these records to a point where we feel they would be acceptable to the world.

Recently I came in contact with a group of men who are accomplishing things on which we have worked for over forty years. Our methods of approach and our formulas are the same. Such things do not just happen. The higher consciousness is fast becoming a world movement. The moment people see the light, they come by many roundabout ways.

QUESTIONS AND ANSWERS

Q. What do the Masters do?

A. They help humanity. That is all that is necessary for them to do. We have seen them feed thousands of people without any outside source of supply visible. They just hand out what is needed.

Q. When are you going to get some pictures of these Masters for your books?

A. We are in hopes that as our planned trip goes forward, we shall be able to bring you the voice and moving pictures of Emil.

Q. Somehow it seems that the Masters inspire us.

A. The greatest inspiration is being one with them. But thoughts are greater than words. We open the way for negative thoughts and we are not strong enough to get rid of them. Yet we can be as busy as can be and still present the Christ. If we worship perfection, it cannot help but come about.

Q. What is the proper medium for the awakening?

A. The individual awakening. As it is with the individual, it is with the group; as it is with the group, it is with the nation; as it is with the nation, it is with the world.

Q. Will you tell about how your family first met Emil?

A. My great-grandfather met Emil soon after he first went to India, and became very intimate with him because of an incident. My great-grandfather was in an expedition going along a regular highway. A man rode up and suggested that they turn off the main highway onto another route. My great-grandfather thought this was peculiar but asked no questions, following the suggestion of this man who accompanied them. The next morning this man left the party. A few days later the news came that a bandit band had come down on the highway they had been following at a time and place where they would have been had they followed their original course. Because of that incident my great-grandfather kept in touch with the man and my family has kept in touch with him ever since. That man is over five hundred years of age. My family has a record of him for over three hundred years. The records show him to be over five hundred. If a man can live five hundred years, he can live five thousand. Emil does not look to be a day over forty.

Q. Why is it that Emil hasn't ascended? He could, couldn't he?

A. Yes. Anyone can. But it isn't a question of taking your body out of a condition where it can be of most service to humanity. The life of the Masters is one of service to humanity, and they don't do anything to disturb life.

Q. As I understand it, the Masters could ascend as well as did Jesus.

A. The body of Jesus was changed before it was nailed to the cross. He knew that they couldn't harm Him. Jesus knew definitely that they could take that body and destroy it and that He could reassemble it. His act was to show that to the people; that there isn't anything miraculous, but that it is a perfectly natural condition. You could take your body any place you desired right tonight if you projected your vision to that place. If you manifest in a spiritual condition, instantly when you project you are there. It is necessary for a person to have a name for an accomplishment, but that accomplishment may be viewed in a million ways.

Q. Do you consider that Jesus completed his work?

A. He not only completed it—He is here today in the same body that was nailed to the cross. The data hasn't been contradicted in twenty years.

Q. How do you explain the statement, "My God, my God, why hast Thou forsaken me?"

A. This is a mistranslation. The words actually were: "My God, my God, Thou hast never forsaken me or any of Thy children, for Thy children can come to Thee as I have come. They can see my life as

I have lived my life. Thus, by living that life, they do incorporate the Christ and become One with Thee, God my Father."

The translators didn't understand many of the words and guessed at many of them. Thus we have the mistranslations. A true Bible could be put out today if it weren't for the disturbing of the people's thoughts. It will come about gradually, until the people accept the records.

Q. Tell us of the separation of planets. Is that the way you account for the distribution of life on other planets?

A. With the right conditions, life could spring up on any planet. Each planet is born from the sun and goes on until human life develops on it. Human life is exactly similar to a planet and is capable of expressing all life. Man has lowered himself by the thoughts he has taken and has been held in the conditions of today, becoming subservient instead of a Master. Really, everything is accomplished, and all man has to do is to accept it.

[UNTITLED]

SCIENCE AND living go hand in hand. Scientists have made many statements which they later found were not facts. They erred because they did not recognize that there is but one principle. Science will no longer be scholarly guesswork when scientists begin to correlate all conditions to that one principle. The discoveries of scientists today are so close to the truth that there are no actual discrepancies. We look forward to the day when this will be apparent to all.

Photography is playing a great part in demonstrating these truths. I want to tell you of some of the advancements that have occurred which I witnessed on my recent trip to India.

There are great people living there who are not only more than five hundred years old, but actually three and four thousand years old. I do not blame you if you are mystified and question my statements. But the facts are true, even if a skeptical Western world does not accept them. You do not need to take my word for it. I merely am attempting to tell you how these people live and how they accomplish their purposes.

Many people ask me the purpose of living hundreds of years. Now if you could live a thousand years and be just as young as you wish, wouldn't you have a wonderful fund of information at your command? Couldn't you be of great assistance to humanity?

Unless you have been an outstanding person, your life is quickly forgotten after you pass through the change we call death. That very forgetfulness is a drain on humanity. The influence of a person that has been forgotten becomes more or less dormant even though it actually carries on. The memory does not go back to bring that influence into perfect conformity to the completion of humanity.

We are here to bring civilization to a point from which it will never go back into darkness. We are to rise completely out of limitation. The experiments which we were privileged to witness show the great strides being made toward the completion and stepping forth of this race into the seventh stage of its development.

In the Bose Institute it has been demonstrated that photographs can be taken of the single cell, of that cell as it divides and builds another cell, then all taking their place and function in the body. There are billions of cells built every moment. As the cell divides and creates a new cell, our thought is implanted upon it.

In the first cell, all is perfect. That cell was first known as the Christ cell. It is always just as young as ever it was. It never takes on old age. It is the primal spark of life. When we implant in it our thoughts of limitation or old age, or any condition outside of perfection, the body responds. Cells born from the first cell take on its image. Originally it is the image and likeness of God. It is perfect in every way. But it becomes the form we carry in our minds.

Can't we see, if we carry the image of perfection

always, what that will do for these cells? It will build perfection. When we make a success of perfection, we add energy to our bodies. Dr. Bose* says that if we are expending our energy for imperfection, the efficiency of the body can be stepped up 200 percent by turning the energy into the channels of perfection. We can go on just as we are, but isn't it really better to live a definite life? There is so much ahead of us if we will but change our thoughts.

Jesus has lived the most scientific life of which we know. His life has been to show that everyone can accomplish just as He did. Our trouble has been that we have not taken the time to understand His simple teachings. We have always looked for the spectacular — someone to stick pins in his flesh, be buried alive, or suspend animation. But such demonstrations do humanity no good. If the accomplishment is not along scientific lines such that it can be used for everyday purposes, it has no value to individuals. The most valuable thing to humanity is the simple truth by which we can live every day and use every moment of our lives.

It is a most remarkable privilege when we learn how to use thought in our lives. Dr. Bose remarked, "What an age we are living in! What an age of simplicity we are coming to! And what a privilege to live this life and see humanity out of the rut of poverty and distress. I can see the whole world lifting itself out of limitation by the use of thought."

*Sir Jagadis Chandra Bose of the Bose Research Institute, Calcutta.

Dr. Bose shows that we can control every part of the plant life. He proves that there is not a plant in existence that did not come into manifestation through the thoughts of man. Man has built it all. It is that God principle flowing through humanity that brings into being this beauty we see in nature.

He makes the statement that if it were not for the human family, there would be nothing in existence today—not even the animals. If there were no fear in the hearts of humanity, there would not be a carnivorous animal in existence, or an animal that fights another. We know that the fiercest animal will not harm us if we do not fear it. Unless we emit fear, that animal will pass by us just as it passes the trees or grass. It is often said that if you love an animal, it will always be your friend and protector.

*   *   *

When the medicine man takes up his work, he must perform his healings instantly. It is a silent ceremony. We saw twelve men go to the medicine man's tent for healing, none of them staying more than one minute, and all came away healed. We have seen the same things in India. We can trace and verify instantaneous healings in this country.

Our great trouble comes from the fact that we allow our thought to scatter. They have a very effective method of teaching in India. The child is placed before a canvas on which there is a single black dot. The child is directed to focus his vision on that dot, and in that condition his problem is presented. Jesus taught that principle — complete concentration on God. When the Hindu beholds the pyramid, he looks from the large end to the point. We look from the point to the large end, allowing our vision to scatter. Just try to hold your vision to a certain point for several moments. Then let it go from side to side and back to that point again. By that exercise you tone up the optic nerve. Likewise, you can centralize your thought on a point of the body, thereby bringing energy to that point and taking it out of any condition of imperfection.

QUESTIONS AND ANSWERS

Q. Are the Masters reincarnated?

A. They talk very little about reincarnation. It isn't necessary for them to be reincarnated.

Ascension is only the ascension of the thoughts. If we vision a place where we would like to be and yet remain here, it is our own thoughts that keep us here. Instantly we vision a better condition, we could be in that condition instantly. We have seen the Masters manifesting not only in one body but in three bodies.

We have one instance where a body has lain inactive for six years, and it is in just as good a state of preservation as ever.

Q. You say there is an individual in India you know as Jesus. I realize the Christ in me, and I would like to contact the personality of Jesus.

A. You are making an idol of the personality. You don't need to present the personality to present the Christ.

Q. What about death?

A. No one ever died who didn't choose to die. We have been told that we must die, but God never told us so.

Q. Tell us about reincarnation.

A. It is a remedy for the mistake of death. It is a light on the blind path of death. To the Masters, it is not necessary. They accomplish everything right here in this life. There really is no death. It is a mistake. We can prove that photographically. There is never a cessation of life. Consequently there could be no death. There is no one to make the choice for you. There is no question but that every individual makes the choice. It looks on the photographs as though at the moment the life element leaves the body and goes on, it begins to assemble substance and build a new body. It must have intelligence. The soul is only the vehicle of the Spirit. All is Spirit always. If there is Spirit outside of us, there is Spirit within. You can not make a separation, because in making a separation you become divided. If we make no separation, we are always at one with that thing. That is what is known as atonement — at-one-ment. It is the body throwing off the worn-out cells. In that way, we die every instant and resurrect every instant. There is not a body in the world which is over seven years old. It is only the idea we present to the body that gives it the form of age above seven years. We grow in accomplishment, but it is not necessary to take on any other condition. But we do. We will not let this body alone. We see only the conditions which surround us. The instant we project an ideal for ourselves that is higher than that in which we have been living, we have made a complete new body and a new situation for that body. That body is definitely electronic or spiritual, whichever you like to pronounce it. Everything is spiritual. You could not define it as anything else but spiritual and live true to form. You may define it as God, if you wish. It is all exactly the same thing. It is only the thoughts we take for the body that take it out of that condition. In reality, it is never out of that condition.

Q. I believe in being the Christ. But I have always thought of Jesus as being the favored one.

A. Jesus said that had He proclaimed that He was the only Christ, He could not have become the Christ.

You could not say "God" once and have your body function at the same vibrations as before. It is not the word of God but the word *God*. Light and life is all one. You must give it one name always. You can never think of these things but that your body is vibrating at a higher attitude. These things can be reduced to a mathematical formula and I believe that you are going to see that put out within eighteen months. It will be a true mathematical formula that can be worked out whereby the body will fall right into line every time. It will be for all. No one will be able to withhold it when it is worked out. It will be as simple as the mathematical table and it will be used for bodily perfection. It is being worked out right here in the United States.

Q. Do you believe that it is possible now for one to

bring his vibrations up to a point where he can take his physical body with him?

A. Yes. There are hundreds and perhaps thousands who are doing it. I believe it will be worked out that those people are setting up vibrations in their bodies which are greater than gravity.

THE POWER OF THOUGHT

IN THIS work the astonishing part of it is that we are finding groups of people all over the country carrying on this same experimental work, more particularly the conditions that can be brought about by thought.

One group will come out and announce that in their study and experiments they have about determined that thought travels at a rate of speed one thousand times greater than light. That is an astonishing thing. Another thing—it shows us just what we can accomplish through thought, if we will but control thought and the actions pertaining to it.

Now this group have determined fully that a bar of steel being put through the many processes of its development can be changed through the thoughts of the people working it. That is an astonishing condition revealed in the past few months. It shows how we are progressing. It shows the control which we can use. If we can control a bar of steel with our thoughts, how much more we can control our bodies, in every action and vital movement.

Those are not our determinations, but are the determinations of independent groups of people, and scientists working along that line. Today there is beginning the greatest change, with every condition of the human family controlled by thought action. Can not we see where that is taking us; what Jesus meant when He said, "Every thought shall be accounted for"? Can not we see that He lived the most scientific life that we have ever known? Does it not make His life more vital to us and more comprehensive?

Definite thought action—man's complete dominion over every condition, man the lord of the universe complete with the divine Principle. Now the Bible has told us that. Jesus has told us that. Still, we have been in the dark. Today the scientists are bringing it into existence in a perfectly complete way. Their studies are carrying us on to an unfoldment that is greater than any to which we have ever looked forward. Those very conditions on which we have speculated are coming about.

We have been told that they were speculations. Even our churchmen have told us that God was speculation and that there was no basis of conclusion except through faith. Today it is the knowing factor. Jesus explained it when He said, "Make the faith knowing." We are doing that today. We have taken theoretical speculation out into the natural, brought about through man's own thinking.

It is a well-known fact today, proved photographically, that our thoughts control not only the body action but every atom and cell that is created in the body. Now that brings us to another conclusion—that we make a success of everything we undertake. Many make a success of failure. We make a success of it ourselves. Now if we will turn completely with the same attitude of thought, changing it to what Jesus meant by the Truth, we will make a success of perfection, and we cannot fail. Why? Because scientists are telling us that we do nothing to build perfection. It is already built. The only condition is to work definitely and become one with that perfection — definite thought action — definite principle. Never wavering, we cannot but succeed.

Scientists are telling us that we use 96.4% of our energy in negative thinking, thus taking perfection out of our body and giving it to the negative thinking. There has been deep study on that, and it has been proved conclusively. We bring into existence this psychic condition, this turmoil and dissolution we think we are in. Today it can be proved that it is only a psychic condition. Where does it come from? We have taken it from our body, thereby building up a hypnotic influence. It can be dissolved instantly. Jesus said that it can be accomplished in the twinkling of an eye. Does that say that it will take years? No. It can be done instantly, and it can be shown photographically.

What did Jesus say positive thoughts are? "I am," not "I will." With that statement He covered every condition. When He said that the truth makes you free, He knew full well that the truth or positive thoughts freed you of a negative condition. It is wholly up to the individual whether he returns to the negative or not. Jesus said, "I go always forward." Did He ever look back? Was it sacrilege when He said, "I am God"? He knew the scientific fact back of it. He was in contact with the condition that has always existed, and He lived by it.

Greater civilizations than ours have lived by it. But they began to see dual. Then what happened? Duality began to take energy from their bodies to keep duality in existence, and immediately that energy was flowing from their bodies to their own thoughts, building up the psychic condition.

There is a great impetus swinging thought back into its perfect condition where our dominion lies. And it is not through some spectacular experience. No one ever saw Jesus come forward in any spectacular condition. It has always been a quiet, determined movement in the right direction. We are going back to the scientific value of thought, showing photographically how it operates.

There is a camera in existence which exposes three films at once. Before that camera we seat three people. One is a person who can think definitely in one direction. Another takes a more or less neutral attitude, allowing conditions to flow through his thought. The other thinks negatively, allowing himself to stay under this hypnotic influence. What happens? In less than one minute the body of the person thinking definitely begins to show in light upon the film. There is a very slight light surrounding the one thinking neutrally. In the case of the person thinking negatively, there is no change. When completed, the picture of the person thinking definitely stands out in a blaze of light.

We find that the body of the person thinking definitely is the true body. That true body is a Light Body, and it always emits light. It may be kept in direct line with perfection at all times. Nothing can touch it.

Just lately we saw the experiment tried. That person got up from his chair and took three thousand volts of electrical energy. The vibration of his body was so high that the current flowed through his body doing no harm whatsoever. There was nothing spectacular about the experiment. It was done scientifically. It means this: that it is proved that this body is indestructible if you take the right attitude of thought and train the body to produce those thoughts.

It is a simple process. It may seem complex until we understand it. It can be traced directly back to the lesson of the crucifixion. The crucifixion was not a spectacular display. It was a test, and Jesus knew that He was going through it. Therefore He could say, "I am about my Father's business." He knew that He worked with the Father and that the Father and He were one. He went further and said, "I Am God."

Now what did He mean by that? He was using a definite principle for all humanity to use. He knew that humanity had already risen to a high degree through the understanding of that very principle. He was only showing the way. They could take His body and place every limitation upon it, even to putting it into a tomb, yet He could come through it. The emanations were such that they would have burst the rocks of the tomb before the body could have been destroyed. We have seen that condition brought about through laboratory tests, completely proving man's dominion over conditions—man the ruler of the universe completely unlimited.

If we would only get out of this attitude of limitation! As we were told, "Just open your eyes to see." Asking what we would see, we were told, "God." Most of you have heard of Doctor Carrel's book *Man the Unknown*, in which he tells of seeing healings of conditions called unhealable by the medical profession. Even more lately he has told of experiments with people who know how to pray, not in the old beseeching way, but standing in full dominion, and he states that he saw 100% healings.

Now is it not wonderful to have those statements from a man like Dr. Carrel? He probably knows more about the human body than any other man today. Many things about which we have speculated are being taken out of the superhuman and unnatural and placed where they belong, with man in complete command — perfectly natural and perfectly simple. It is simplifying Jesus' teachings so that we can study them in the light in which they belong. Today we are coming back to simplicity in every attitude of thought, without diversity, but in unity with every thought carried to that high point of contact where it accomplishes, needing but one thought to accomplish.

In every root language, although the word for God is spelled differently, the letters have the exact vibratory influence. It was only a short while ago that we thought of God as a great being, set out in the skies, and that we could not find out about Him until we died. Today we are discarding that idea. The result is that we are brought into the knowing attitude. We know that we become that very thing when we stand one with it. The moment we do, our body falls right into line.

I think you have heard me say many times that if we say the word "God" meaningly, reverently and with due thought, the vibrations of our body will never respond to the same influence as before we said that word. It is known today that such a body fills with energy enough to light a twenty-watt globe. That is proof of the building of energy in the body until it overflows. That influence carries out to the multitudes. Jesus knew when He talked to the multitudes that the principle was flowing from His body. Many saw Him standing in a complete blaze of light. How can we doubt for a moment that He did know what He was doing? He was presenting those conditions to humanity to use, and we have been all these years trying to understand them. Now they are coming home to us. We are rising out of the hypnotic condition in which we have surrounded ourselves and of which we made a success which did not satisfy us. In turning to the other, we shall make a greater success. Why? Because it is so much more simple and takes less energy.

It can be shown photographically how each cell is built. The moment a cell divides itself from the parent cell, and the instant before it divides itself, it takes on the exact image of the parent. As it goes out, it comes under the influence of this imperfection that we think for ourselves. What happens? We see the vibrations of the cell lowered, and in some instances when it attaches itself to the organ where it belongs, it is a dead thing. That cell which started out with all its energy has become a dead cell in less than one second. The very thought influence of imperfection influences that cell until it dies. The vibrations go so low that the dynamic influence flows out. That is where you have the root of every disease.

Now a new body begins to build immediately as a right thought surrounds us. That same life energy can be induced to return. Death as we have known it is not accomplished. This is not the conclusion of only one group, but of many groups. We cannot affect Principle irrespective of the energy we have given to other conditions.

Never in His talks did Jesus mention the devil. It is only ourselves who have built His Satanic Majesty into our consciousness. Where would it get its power? Merely from the individual. But that has not changed Principle. There is no devil; there is no death; there is no damnation. Jesus never used the words and never thought of them, in fact. Such instances as are recorded in the Bible are merely folklore. He never used a negative word or condition and never recognized a power other than God, explaining that humanity had used that great power singly. We are not at a loss any more to explain those conditions. Many people have seen through them, but generally it has been thought to be more or less a visionary condition. At times we get beyond the hypnotic stage, and then a flash of the real comes through. Then we do not hesitate to accept it. Each experience of this kind makes us stronger in acceptance. Then we are "about our Father's business."

When Jesus had multiplied the loaves and the fishes and the people had tried to crown Him king, what did He do? He simply withdrew. He had shown them the way. They must take the next step for themselves. It has taken people two thousands years to recognize it. Scientists are telling us that this principle is even older than humanity and in fact has always existed. "Before Abraham was born, I AM."

It gives us an entirely new light upon the subject, new only to us, since it is the old, old condition brought about by our understanding. We must accomplish for ourselves, standing on our own feet as did Jesus.

QUESTIONS AND ANSWERS

Q. Have we a political leader among us who under-
stands these truths?

A. That I cannot say. But our politics are not going
to keep them away. When our political situation
becomes a failure we rise above it. Jesus said that
every man was king. If we stand in that attitude
politics fall right into line. We are not a flock of
sheep. We do not need to follow.

Q. Will you explain the battle of Armageddon?

A. We fight that every day. If we let go of the material the fight is over.

Q. What will be the fate of the nations which are
drawing away from all religions?

A. Christianity as it was presented to those nations
was not accepted because it was presented with too
much materiality infused in it. But they are going
to find that no nation can live without spirituality. It is the very foundation of every nation. Our
Bible says that God is a spirit. The "a" does not
belong in the statement. God *is* Spirit.

Q. Does your third volume contain the same teaching as the first two volumes?

A. It carries on the earlier teaching to a higher determination. It is the completion of those experiences.

Q. Is the Second Coming of Christ meant to refer to the coming of Christ consciousness or the reappearance of Jesus?

A. He is always on the earth as He was. When man accepts the Christ, he stands face to face with that very thing. It means that Jesus will come forth in bodily form to many more.

Q. Why is it that we know so little about the Masters who are working among us?

A. It is because they work quietly. A Master does not need to advertise Himself. We still have the first one to say to us that He is a Master. They are of the people as much as anyone else.

Q. How long will it be before the denominational hatreds of the world are dissolved?

A. We cannot determine that. It is wholly with the people themselves. If they draw apart, there is an eventual submergence. A body is but represented by the units of that body. When people are ready for a better condition, they shall be joined to it.

Q. Why do not the churches send people to learn about all this instead of teaching hell and damnation?

A. They are seeing the change and attempting to cooperate. There is a definite attempt for the union of thought. People today are coming much closer than in the past. They see that it will be necessary to cooperate or be isolated. We can help them by the attitude we take.

Q. Is it necessary to go through death and reincarnations?

A. It is not necessary if we accomplish all in this life, and we can if we will. But if we make the mistake of what we call death, there is a remedy which is called reincarnation. Before the life element leaves the body, the choice is made, and that choice comes about by the definite attitude we take in this life.

Q. Is it not true that we are all Masters in a degree?

A. We are not only Masters in a degree, but we are wholly Masters if we determine in that way. We could not even think of it if it were not already accomplished for us.

THE POWER OF POSITIVE THINKING

WHEN STATEMENTS are made in a positive, determined manner, their accomplishment is unlimited. We can show the scientific value of positive thought and the stating positively of condition. It can be proved that back of every positive statement is a working principle or truth.

Therefore we can readily see what Jesus meant when He said, "The Truth makes you free." It was not promised for the future, as "The Truth will make you free," as it has been erroneously translated, but as a definite statement in the present tense. We find that the most definite statement that humanity can use is that statement so often read, "I Am God." The statement, "I am not God," having no positive force and truth, does not belong to humanity. Positive declarations free us from negative conditions. In the original language there was never a negative word nor a past tense. Every negative word in the language was injected into it long after the language was born.

The language that Jesus used contained no negative words. He lived always in the present with no negative thoughts, accomplishing in that definite, positive declaration. Looking at these facts, we can see how one would accomplish, knowing that back of every pronouncement is a positive, definite force that brings that pronouncement into existence.

These simple principles are so definitely presented in the new attitude of thought that the whole human family is waking to them. We find that the human race in ancient times learned to use these principles. That influence never ceased, and as humanity presents the ideal today, that influence gathers force.

We have carried out experiments with photography whereby we see definitely how hypnotic, negative situations deceive the eye but not the camera. Irrespective of any seeming condition, there was never anything created by a negative thought. Negative thought begets a hypnotic influence, and where that influence is used to create an effect, that effect cannot be photographed.

Negative thinking takes energy from the body, whereas positive thinking adds and creates energy. Scientists tell us that if there were one atom out of place in the universe, the whole universe would fly apart. Every human body is a universe, containing a solar sun. We have forgotten our birthright; we are hypnotized into a condition in which we do not believe. Without belief there can be no creative power. Although we refuse to harmonize with the principle, we cannot be taken out of it. It is necessary only to review the above thought to have harmony reassert itself.

QUESTIONS AND ANSWERS

Q. Can we help to eliminate Karma from the minds of others and how?

A. The greatest assistance we know is to see others standing forth definitely as the Christ.

Q. There are so many different teachings, and while they all hinge on the Christ, they approach the subject in different ways. Can you tell us the best way to take up the teachings?

A. We have no method of teaching. Of course there are many attitudes of thought, and that is the reason for the different teachings. Do they not all point to the same thing?

Q. Some teachings point to the present and some to the future. What is the ultimate goal?

A. In reality is not perfection in existence already? If we would accept it, that is all that is necessary. I have no choice of lessons to make for you, but it appears to me that they all bring us to the point of acceptance. There are many attitudes of thought, and it may be necessary for one group to take one series of lessons and for another group to take another series. If we look to perfection as in the future, where would we accomplish it? I feel that we can all make the determination that perfection is here and now and accept it, regardless of any lessons.

Q. Isn't it true that Paul did not attain the Christ consciousness?

A. If Paul was struggling to attain the Christ consciousness, he had not attained it. Anyone works face to face and side by side with Jesus if he presents the Christ. Had Paul ascended to the mastership, he would not have been a disciple any more.

Q. What is the woman's part in this new age?

A. Just as much as that of a man. We are all one. The male and the female are one. They only separate themselves. There is no separation in Spirit. All is Spirit.

Q. To whom do you pray?

A. To God, presenting God to the world. We do not pray to an outside deity. If there is an outside deity, that deity must be within. Your life is a prayer. It isn't mere words. Consequently, by the reduction of prayer to mere words we fail in the accomplishment.

Q. What about healing?

A. There is no healing. Healing is a name for a condition that comes about. You can not keep perfection away if you allow it to come to you.

101

Q. Isn't the deity three?

A. Where would you find three if it is within yourself? It would be only the deity you make if you make a division.

Q. Could there be such an ideal situation as the complete change of our monetary system to the extent that no money would be used?

A. We do not look forward to such a condition. In our economic system, money is necessary. But you will see it so plentiful that people will not put the same value upon it. There will be a general distribution, not for gain but for service.

Q. Can you tell us something of the life of Jesus from the twelfth to the thirtieth years?

A. We know positively that He spent the last nine of these years in India. Evidently He went about from place to place seeing a great deal of the things He later taught. Suddenly we find Him standing forth, showing all humanity that it could accomplish just as He did. He lived that life to show mankind that it could present the same condition and live by it.

Q. Did Jesus suffer bitter anguish on the cross?

A. In all probability, no. We were told that He was far beyond suffering. He showed all humanity that man could put any limitation on His body and He could rise above it.

Q. When you were with Jesus, did He give you any *special* message?

A. No. We have many messages He gave us. The messages in the books were presented with the thought that we could give them out as we wished. None of His messages were exclusive in any way. We have never found Him working exclusively.

SPIRITUAL HARMONY

I HAVE REFERRED before to the Temple of Silence in which we saw so many remarkable healings. We were told that if a piece were chipped from this building, it would renew itself immediately. Such an accomplishment has been photographed, and we have seen the human body renewed in the same manner and by the same principle, but in even greater degree.

Why is it that we do not respond instantly to these conditions when even inanimate objects do so? It is because we have hypnotized ourselves into disbelief. It is because of the lack of acceptance that humanity has lost its heritage.

The power is just as evident and potent now as it ever was, and every human being can use it. It is the power that produces so-called healings, which are not healings in reality, but acceptance of that perfection that is never in any way changed. When we accept perfection, we are out of the condition of imperfection. It is the natural thing for humanity; it belongs to humanity; it is humanity's highest attribute. If we would let go of the condition with which we have surrounded ourselves when we have allowed imperfection to express, perfection would come forth so dynamically we could not express an inharmonious word. That is the only necessary condition for humanity to

become completely perfect — to make this body indestructible, pure and in evidence at all times, never
veiled in mystery or outside of itself or incomplete.

This body has a central sun around which every
atom revolves. Each atom itself has a solar sun around
which the atoms revolve. When we stand completely
immersed in that declaration, we can make it as simple as "I Am God." With that, not only every atom,
but the solar sun of every atom begins to emit light,
and the moment that light appears, every atom shows
itself to be in complete harmonious accord. The moment light begins to appear and those atoms begin to
glow, there is not a semblance of inharmony in the
body. It is completely healed.

Thus it is that each one can not only heal himself,
but can bring himself directly into spiritual harmony
and accord with the Universal, and one knowing that
can say, "If your eye be single your whole body is filled
with light," and that light is the light that lights every
man who comes into the world.

Each person can declare these conditions for himself, and by that declaration he assists every other person to that same declaration. Although that person to
whom the influence is directed may accept it unknow-
ingly at first, through that acceptance inharmony is
swept away. And so it is not selective. It is in complete
accord — complete unison.

QUESTIONS AND ANSWERS

Q. There are some here who have not studied metaphysical teachings, who are not satisfied with the
orthodox teachings.

A. It is not necessary to renounce anything. If the
orthodox teaching is not to your liking, put a better thought in its place. It may suit millions of
people, but if it does not suit you, put a better
thought in its place. It is for the individual to
present a higher attitude and a higher condition
and then things fall into line always.

Q. Can you give God a definition?

A. By giving God a definition we localize him. We say
people are in orthodoxy. Isn't it our fault that they
are? It isn't what the other fellow does. It is what
we do. The person in orthodoxy may be well satisfied. If they are not satisfied, they are looking to
a higher situation. They are perfecting an ideal
for them to follow. They must go on with that perfection and become one with that ideal. You may
call that metaphysics if you wish. It does not need
a name. It needs an attitude of thought toward
the accomplishment.

Q. Do the Masters precipitate their food?

A. We do not look upon these things as precipitation.

The food is there instantly. There is nothing said about it. We sat down at the table and the containers were filled, and as we used what was in them they were filled as many times as necessary. We have never been able to bring anything about so that we could photograph it stage by stage. It would *seem* that it came through the method of precipitation. It was there instantly as we could see it.

Q. Was the Jew responsible for the crucifixion of Jesus?

A. We do not put that at the door of any nationality at all. Had He not wished to present a condition through which all men could go, they could not have crucified Him. It was a definite method to show His people that they could go through these conditions without the least effect upon themselves. Had it not been for that purpose, He could have taken His body and gone on with it as He showed many times. It was not a thing imposed upon Him except that He allowed the imposition for a purpose.

Q. Can you tell us some method for attaining Mastership?

A. There is no formula. It is wholly in the determination of the individual himself. The greatest presentation of Mastership to us is the statement of Jesus, "Behold, Christ is here." The moment we present Christ and live that life, we are a Master. Then we are a Master of every situation and every condition. It is a perfectly simple declaration. It is the person presenting the Christ to the world. As Jesus often says, "The greatest sermon ever preached was 'Behold God.'" How could there be a greater sermon?

Q. Where was Jesus for the fifty years after His crucifixion?

A. He was with His disciples. He is still in the same body as He always was.

PRINCIPLE IN ACTION

WHY IS IT," I am frequently asked, "that with all of the lofty philosophy in India, people do not overcome their poverty?"

India is a land of seeming contradictions. One can prove or disprove anything by tales, beliefs and observations drawn from this far-off land. A trivial discussion over a dinner table brought this home. Among others, there were guests from Kashmir, Bengal, and Burma.

One said, "I didn't want to go to India because of the tigers there."

Another countered, "Why, I saw no tigers in India."

The other answered, "Well, we see tigers every day in India."

Each had lived in a different part of the country, and each stated a particular truth for his section which did not necessarily hold for the entire land. This observation applies to many of the half-truths and localized opinions which we hear on every side.

We have carried on a great deal of work to show Principle in action. Churchmen have said, "Why, this is only a faith, and faith is only speculation. Spirit is but a speculative principle concerning the passing existence of man." These men held important offices in their organizations, and yet they were inclined to vague and evasive statements.

There is a new spirit at work in the churches today, especially among the younger generation. They are seeking to express a new attitude toward religion. These do not belong just to one group or country. They are found in all walks of life.

These far-seeing souls feel that they belong to humanity rather than to any separative group. This feeling of unity is the very rock upon which the church was originally established. It was not a "house of clay and stone," but a Spiritual Fact, solid, never changing.

Recall how science has changed in twenty years. Many of their precepts have undergone complete change. They are coming nearer and nearer to the principle which is all-pervading. Scientists are admitting that there is one definite principle upon which everything is based, and out of which everything is born. When they discover the nature of the principle, science will not have to change or retrace its steps any more, but will, from then on, go forward with greater clearness of perception toward undreamed-of goals.

The early churches were known as "assemblies." Today the church should be an assembly of individuals where people could come together to learn to recognize the spiritual manifestations of Truth and to know how to work with the great principle through which they can accomplish the purpose of life.

Negative suggestions have crept into all groups until they have become saturated with them. A few individuals have always fought and stood firm, knowing that there existed truths for which they should strive. When such faithful ones kept true with the "eye single" to that one principle, they have manifested powers which no outside influence could alter. These state that there is one determining element or principle. Allowing everyone complete freedom of expression, still the body exists in Principle, wherein perfection always has existed and must exist.

QUESTIONS AND ANSWERS

Q. What use would a Master have for a physical body?

A. We do not know, but we do know that they use them at times. In all probability it is so that they can approach and teach people. They put no thought on the body since the body takes care of itself. Many of them have sat and eaten with us, but in all probability it was for sociability only.

Q. What determines the time between passing and rebirth?

A. We know of no definite time. In all probability the person passing through the experience of death chooses a very definite path to rebirth instantly before death comes out. We believe that some choose a longer period because they have some condition which they want to work out, while others choose to come back in a very short time.

Q. Was Jesus of a different material than we are and did He have a different privilege and was He of God and was not His life to show that we have the same privilege?

A. He lived to show us, and He attempted to teach the whole world that all mankind had the same

112

privilege and that if one man could accomplish it, all can and will. The New Testament, correctly translated, has these precepts in it.

Q. Why has the record of Jesus' life since the crucifixion been kept secret?

A. There is no attempt on the part of the people who have the records to keep them secret. The Western world does not come in close contact with those things, partly because they are not advertised and partly because of the disbelief of the people.

Q. Orthodox churches teach that Christ is coming again, manifesting on this earth.

A. He has always manifested on this earth. The Second Coming evidently meant that when all present and know the Christ, He does appear.

Q. Is it an error for the human mind to confine the Christ to Jesus?

A. He said, "I see the Christ in every face and in every form. When the first man was born, the Christ was born."

Q. If we perfect ourselves in this lifetime, is it necessary to return through reincarnation?

A. No.

Q. If Jesus is here in body, why does not He appear and declare Himself so that all would know Him?

A. He does present Himself so that all can know Him,

but will all know Him? The way is open, and if all presented the Christ, all would stand face to face with the Christ. The one who presents Him is the one who sees Him.

THE ENDOCRINES

(Comment: The editors of Mind Magazine *have been in possession of these very interesting questions and answers for some time but have withheld publication until our readers might have an opportunity of following carefully the many other aspects of Mr. Spalding's teaching as presented during the past two years in this periodical. *)*

TODAY WE have somewhat of a technical subject which is, however, one of very great importance to all, as it deals with the scientific side of spiritual development.

The thyroid controls the whole endocrinal system, bringing it into harmony with all of the other glands and the whole glandular system. It is through this development that the spiritual faculties are brought into conscious use. That is, through the stimulation of the thyroid the spiritual faculties are brought out and correlated.

Q. Will you please enumerate the glands for the benefit of those of us who are not familiar with physiology?

A. There are seven of these glands: The pineal, the

*[i.e. 1935-37]

pituitary, the thyroid, the thymus, the pancreas, the adrenals and the gonads. The thyroid is the most important. It straddles the trachea, with two lateral lobes and one central lobe.

The gonads dominate between 14 and 45. The thyroid especially dominates from 45 onward. It doesn't begin to function until the advent of puberty. The pineal is more or less active until that period of life. The true outer function of the pineal is to delay the advent of puberty until about the 14th year, or until the body becomes strong enough. Many children have more or less spiritual vision for that reason. Many children have very remarkable spiritual insight during their earlier years until this period is reached.

Q. What methods do the Masters use in stimulating the function of the thyroid?

A. Later in life they use a method of stimulating its action by centering on the thyroid. This brings it into physical activity, and it begins to develop to a greater extent right along, feeding the body until it becomes regenerated. They do not use chemicals at all. It is solely by the concentration of thought upon it.

Q. What is the influence of oxygen from a Master's standpoint?

A. If it is inhaled in a natural way through the breath, it has the greatest stimulating influence. They do not give it otherwise. They give exercises to stimulate the respiratory organs in order to take in and assimilate more and more oxygen all of the time.

Q. The control of the body is, as we understand it, through the thyroid in relation to this respiration of the body — the influence of the thyroxin.

A. Yes. It plays a very important part in the oxidation of the material that is thrown off, and also in the bringing of the oxygen into a condition through which the body can use it, putting it into the bloodstream as well.

Q. What is the influence attained through the interstitial cells of the gonads that brings about rejuvenation which you cannot bring about by an increased activity of the thyroid? There must be some way known to bring about a rejuvenation of the body by increasing the activity of the thyroid, but already marked evidences of rejuvenation have been accomplished through the interstitial gonads, by gland transplantation, and by the ligation method of Stinach.

A. Still there is no permanent rejuvenation in that way. But where your thyroid is brought to a certain activity — to the point where spiritual perception takes place — you have your rejuvenation that becomes active and permanent. Your rejuvenation is then permanent.

You will find that in gland transplantation, or in any purely physical method, there is a breaking-down period, whereas with the spiritual development there is no such breaking down at all. Where rejuvenation is brought about through the development and use of the thyroid in connection with spiritual activity, it is evidently permanent. There is no need to resort to the gonads at all.

They claim in the East that the spiritual activity can be carried right on from youth. They give specific training to a considerable extent in that. Even in Calcutta University it is known as spiritual transmutation.

Q. Is Emil in a body that has lasted him four hundred years?

A. Yes. Over four hundred years. It is apparently as young as it ever was.

Q. How does that body differ in the texture of the flesh?

A. It is finer. You would recognize a finer condition, but at the same time there is no difference really in the cellular construction, apparently. Although a higher state of vibration is maintained, you are not so conscious of this as you are of the facial expression that is immediately noticeable. There is not a sign of old age.

Usually the hands are the first sign of old age, and their hands never show any age. Then, of course, there is no facial expression of old age. The hair is well preserved. In many of them the hair is never gray.

Q. Take some of the younger individuals that you have mentioned who are about 75 or 80 years of age, and look their age, and changes come about in them so that in the course of a few years they become 40 or 50. Was the influence spiritual, and was it working through the endocrine system?

A. As soon as the spiritual understanding is stimulated to any extent, the endocrine system begins to operate, and, as they say, it comes into its own proper activity. It is just harmonized and speeded up in its action. Each individual still moves in the direction of creating this youth. We have seen that accomplished in a very short time. We had one very remarkable instance.

One of the old coolies who was with my grandfather and who at that time was an old man, came and asked to go with us on one of our expeditions. I said, "No, you are too old." Emil heard me turn down his request and said, "Let him go, if he wants to." Upon his return, his friends failed to recognize him. His hair was dark, and he had lost his age completely. He was an ordinary coolie for all that we knew, travel-worn and quite decrepit before setting out. He is still living and retains his youthful appearance to this day.

Q. Then one method of rejuvenating the thyroid after the age of 45 is to feed the physical body on vitamin-producing food?

A. Yes. It all helps at the beginning.

Q. Is there, then, some association between prana and the vitamins?

A. There is a very close relationship and association. It brings into activity the hormones of the body. The vitamins bring the hormones into activity and increase them.

Q. Are vitamins more physical than chemical?

A. Yes. They are enzymes and, therefore, catalyzers.

Q. Let us relate this subject to fear. In 1918, during the great "flu" epidemic, was not fear at the bottom of its continuance?

A. As soon as fear subsided, the epidemic subsided also. If fear is overcome completely, the thyroid will be undisturbed by any negative emotions. Love overcomes fear completely and stimulates the action of the thyroid gland immediately.

Q. I have heard of many fakirs and of some men of real spiritual attainment who have eaten nails, glass and poisons of various sorts, and have survived for a time, and then, suddenly, collapsed. They would go on, perhaps, for months or years, apparently unharmed. X-rays would show no sign of things eaten but a few moments previously. What caused the ultimate collapse, in those cases where it has occurred?

A. The cause is primarily egotism. When an individual comes to the point where he is hypnotized into believing that he is the power which performs so-called miracles — when his personality asserts itself beyond the Christ Within in conscious activity —

the thyroid ceases to secrete and distribute the antitoxin. Nothing else will destroy the function of the thyroid gland so readily as egotism, which destroys all spiritual activity.

RISING OUT OF LIMITATION

IF WE saw a person hold out his hand when he needed bread, and instantly a loaf of bread would appear in that hand, we should stand in great awe. This would seem to the Western mind to be a miracle contrary to nature. But upon close study, we see that it is fully possible for everyone to achieve similar phenomena. We have everything that belongs to us. All is here, and we do not bring it from anywhere else. All is accomplished. We need only to project the acceptance and it is ours to use.

I have mentioned often the so-called fakirs in India who apparently throw a rope into the air, call a boy from the audience and have him climb up the rope. The boy usually disappears at the top, but sometimes instead of disappearing, the boy will remain visible at the top of the rope. The fakir in a seeming rage climbs after the boy, cuts off his arms and legs, only later to repent and put him back together again.

When we attempt to photograph these seeming events, nothing is recorded on the film. What happened? We have studied the phenomena and learn that there are twelve stages of hypnotic influence. The fakir can project the pictures so rapidly and definitely that the audience will accept them as reality.

* * *

That started an entirely new field of research. Now, through the use of a certain ray we can so irradiate a plot of ground that after twenty-four hours we can plant a kernel of corn which will develop into a fully grown stalk with two completed ears upon it within seven minutes. Another group has been able to develop a bearing grapefruit tree in six months, whereas it usually takes six years.

Carrying on the experiment, we planted a kernel of corn in a plot of ground that had not been irradiated in this way to observe its growth photographically. Whereas the growth of the latter is at the rate of nine million cells per second, the growth of the former is at the rate of ninety-six billion cells per second. All we have succeeded in doing is to accelerate nature. There has been no unnatural miracle about it.

The same principle is involved as when the disciples said to the Master that there was need of food and that it was still four months till the harvest. Jesus said, "Look upon the fields, they are white to harvest." We have always pronounced that a miracle. But Jesus explained that it was no miracle and that the slow process we accept as natural is not natural. We in our lack of progress put nature back to where it responds to our limitations. Someone has told us that it takes four months to grow corn and six years to grow a grapefruit. Today it is known that if we release those limitations, nature springs into existence immediately.

Now these experiments are expensive, and it is not known how soon they will prove to be practical for everybody. But we can envision that it will be. I can remember when aluminum was worth $450.00 per ounce. Today it is a common product. The same thing takes place in every line of endeavor. Many of the great conditions have been in existence all along, but it takes people a long time to realize that they themselves are putting on the limitations. Usually experimental work is done in the wrong way. We set up certain conditions, believing that they will accomplish certain results. Today we are going to the result instead of the experiment, knowing first that it has all been worked out in nature and is in existence.

You can leave a seed in a metal receptacle and it will not germinate unless someone comes along who can present life to it. It is known today that there are people who can so project life that it will penetrate every substance. The moment the seed comes in contact with the life emanation that has been put forth, you can observe that vibration dropping right down to the heart of that seed where it begins the process of growth. There is a man on the Pacific Coast who can germinate life in seeds to 90 percent where before the percentage was only 30 percent. Experiments are being made with soil whereby production can be stepped up considerably more.

We put the limitations on nature. Nature works in complete harmony with us, and that harmony is instantaneous when we allow the response to come forth. There is not a blade of grass, not a tree, not a flower in existence but that it came into existence first through the projection of life from the individual.

There is an artist who has made some remarkable experiments. He paints on his canvas the color he wants the plant before him to take on, and as a result we have some of the most beautiful flowers. Then he can take a cactus and place it in a glass case. He sits before it and tells it that it is now protected and does not need its spines and should just let them drop off. Finally the cactus loses its spines.

We say that God grows the trees. God does, but it takes the expression emanating from the individual to start it into existence. We accomplish all things. First the acceptance, then take away the barriers to natural progress by letting go of doubt, fear and superstition, and then the fields are white to the harvest.

It can be shown that Jesus knew every one of these conditions and was perfectly familiar with them. He did not hestiate to show all how they could do exactly as He did if they would let go of or forgive the limitations. Why do we carry these limitations with us? It is only through projecting our thoughts through a lower field where we pick up and repeat them until we take a picture instead of realizing the fact.

QUESTIONS AND ANSWERS

Q. You remarked that work had been done in getting photographic evidence of emanations from the body. Are the results of these experiments available to the public?

A. The photographic work along that line is conducted by our own people in our own laboratory near Calcutta, India. They have not been released because it is desired to carry on more definite research before the results are presented to the world. But there is one body in England carrying on that same research. They are working quietly and we have withheld their name — although they have never asked us not to give it out. We have exchanged photographs with them. These show exactly the same conclusions as ours. It is what we call rapid photography, and is beyond what is known today with the so-called "movie camera." The Eastman people are accomplishing a great deal along that line, but it is still experimental with them.

Q. How should I go about selling a gold mine? It is a good mine but I have not been able to dispose of it.

A. When you have taken a firm attitude that it is of

value to someone, that person can't be kept away from you.

Q. Could you get information from the Masters as to the composition of the unknown film over the gold records you mention?

A. They have told us. But what good are names unless we can find out the actual substance? They tell us the names, but we cannot put it together with our limited knowledge of chemistry today. But every one of the formulae they have given us has eventually worked out.

Q. How can we help friends who are ill?

A. There could be no illness unless man gave it expression. We help hold ourselves and others in any condition that we express.

It would be far better to use the energies of sympathy to build ideas of health and perfection. You can help your friends by encouraging them to build within themselves the perfect thoughts, that they may express that perfection outwardly.

Q. How can I get rid of fear?

A. Just forgive that fear. Fear usually is an attitude that man assumes with things he does not understand. If you will realize that the strength of God is within you and that nothing can harm the essential nature of the real you, all sense of fear will pass away from you.

127

ETERNAL YOUTH

WHEN A child is born we begin at once to impute to it a limitation of three score and ten years. In doing so, we are building into that child a condition not represented in truth. If, instead of placing old age as our goal, we place youth as our goal and step forward in a determined, positive attitude, we would reach it.

It is a well-known fact that men and women are accomplishing in that way today — accomplishing eternal youth. Our great scientists are saying that there is not a human body in existence that is over seven years old. It can be shown that every cell is changed within nine and four-tenths months, every cell changed and every cell a complete young unit.

Many are actually presenting youth, beauty, purity and perfection as their goal. The Western world, however, has made old age very largely the ideal of accomplishment. Were we to worship youth as definitely as we worship old age, we would accomplish it; in fact we could not accomplish anything contrary to it.

This is not an attempt to decry old age. In India, where we know definitely of individuals living hundreds of years, we find them held in reverence, not for the old age they represent but for the youth and beauty they express.

We see many so-called cures. They are but the

acceptance of that perfection which belongs to every individual when he rids himself of that condition that has kept perfection from him. When perfection floods in, it expresses itself without any thought upon the part of the person affected save as he turns from that which has kept perfection away.

No one accomplishes anything unless he becomes one with that accomplishment, forgetting, for a time at least, all other conditions. If we state definite, positive facts for ourselves to accomplish, we do accomplish them readily by never alowing the thought to vary to any negative condition. This principle works with every attitude of positive thought.

The Masters teach that there is no phenomenon regarding healings or any of the other manifestations that may seem miraculous to us. They say that if we observe closely, we will notice that perfection exists in every form, in every atom, in every cell, in every attitude of thought. We only allow ourselves to become accustomed to other conditions — conditions that have no reality.

QUESTIONS AND ANSWERS

Q. If Jesus is living in His body today, what has become of the disciples?

A. Three of them are living and with Him. We do not know of the others. Just as long as they were disciples, they could follow; but when they became Masters, they did not need to follow. Probably they have all attained. That was what Jesus wanted to present. He wanted to show them that the moment they let go of discipleship, they became Masters. For that reason He said, "Behold, a Christ is here," not referring to Himself at all.

Q. People say that they see the Christ in different ways.

A. It is just the condition you look to. The Christ that you present meets the Christ always.

Q. Why go to India to see the Masters?

A. I have told you time after time that you need not go there to see them.

Q. Could that be explained by saying that we only see the thing that we raise our vibrations to reach?

A. We raise our thoughts to Mastership.

Q. Do the words *I Am* have the same value as the word *God*?

A. They do not have the same influence, but they have a vast influence close to it. You run the danger of getting into a psychic influence with the one, but you get right through it with the one word *God*.

[UNTITLED]

I WISH TO present some of the conditions that we bring upon ourselves:

Firstly, that condition we know as old age. Old age does not exist in actual form in the scheme of this universe. Not being founded in Truth, old age is the result of that which man thinks or presents for himself.

The moment a child is born, we begin to set the limitation of that life at three-score and ten years. But what about the fact that today nearly all of our great medical scientists are saying that there is not a human body in existence over seven years old? They are stating that as an absolute conclusion. It could be shown that a body is not even seven years old, because, in fact, every cell of the body is changed within nine and four-tenths months. Every cell multiplies into new cells, each a complete young unity. The waste elements gradually sloughing away in the course of natural functions find their way back to the body of Mother Earth to await another day of usefulness to man.

* * *

Then there is the problem of the state of health. We have seen many so-called cures. It could be shown that healings are only the acceptance of the perfection which belongs to every individual; the individual has

132

dropped the conditions that kept the perfection from him. The perfection floods in and expresses itself without a thought by the person.

Unconsciously they completely let go of limitation. When they arrive at the goal they have set — be it shrine, tomb, holy relic or what — the perfection manifests. It is evident there could be nothing else happen, for when the conscious mind has accepted the change as accomplished, health has to be expressed.

One early fall morning in New York State, the ground was covered with about two inches of snow. A group of boys were congregated in the schoolyard, and they were attempting to see which one could make the straightest tracks to a tree over in the corner of the yard. Each boy wavered and was called back and another given the opportunity. The last lad came up. He walked directly to that tree and his course did not waver one inch out of a straight line.

That interested me and I said, "How did you do it?"

He replied, "I just saw that tree. I did not pay any attention to my feet or where they were going. I just saw that tree!"

That is the way to accomplish by a simple method. The goal of the tree represented perfection. By keeping his eyes only on the goal, without consciously placing his feet, he went directly in a straight line to the point where his thought was projected.

* * *

We have seen countless healings throughout India. However, in this country, it is evident that some condition keeps away similar blessings. Evidently the bars that are thrown up are the lack of belief or faith.

Perfection always exists in every form. Every atom is perfect. Every cell is organized according to law. The perfections are not attained in our bodies only because we have become accustomed to other conditions — conditions that are not realities at all, conditions that have been separated only by man's idea of them, man's presentation of them. Thus only do we have inharmony and separateness.

Like the boy walking straight to the tree, we must set our ideas on the goal of perfection that we may fulfill the law in ourselves.

QUESTIONS AND ANSWERS

Q. Will you tell us about the man who lost his arm?

A. We were in a party going up the Ganges. There were twenty-six not of our own party with us. We pulled along the bank at ten o'clock and the porters had their lunch. One of them was sleeping and his hand dropped into the water. A crocodile snapped it off. The man jumped ashore and appealed to one individual and walked toward him. By the time he had gotten face to face with this individual, the photographs show that the pain had left and that the blood had stopped flowing. We took successive photographs for forty-five minutes, and for the last eight minutes every photograph showed the hand complete. At two o'clock in the afternoon the man took up his place in the boat. Every white man showed wonderment. There was not a native who wondered at it. They all accepted it. A great many of the party took photographs, and we have their signatures on the photographs.

Q. Is it known when man became conscious of the I AM Presence?

A. When humanity came into existence there was the recognition of the determination. It has always been in existence. We only get out of the sonship attitude because we fall below in thought and self-determination.

Q. Is the Darwin theory correct?

A. No. Man has always been the select. Many believe that the life element was projected on an electron from some other planet to this. It was not an evolution from animal to man. We can show you evidence, although I cannot say it is conclusive, that man was on earth before the animal.

Q. Can the embryo of man be photographed undergoing evolution according to the Darwin theory?

A. Scientists are accepting that that was a mistaken theory. All life takes on from the water and other elements in building the body. There is a determining factor which might be classed as animal, but that is only a conception. In their experiments they did not use high enough magnification to see the whole field at once. It is quite definitely concluded that the animal is using the life that the human refuses to use. The animal uses it to keep that life element in motion.

Q. What is the average time that the spirit is in touch with the natural body?

A. It leaves instantly and evidently has no use for the body it leaves. It seems to seek a better or higher condition for itself. Apparently it ascends voluntarily.

136

Q. Would a Master encourage the giving out of his teachings to the world?

A. We have never found them withholding anything. It is given out freely for all to accept who will. They do not make any distinctions.

MANUSCRIPTS & PAPERS

ORIGINAL OF THE LORD'S PRAYER

(From the records of Jesus' life 50 years after the crucifixion, found in a monastery which they occupied.)

GOD OUR FATHER
You stand revealed to us this day as
The ever-present Principle.
Hallowed be your name;
We know it as Elohim.
Give us to live and know this day as you, God, alone
see us living and knowing,
Ever pure and perfect,
As you have revealed your Perfection to man.
And that Perfection has come forth as your son,
your only creation,
The only one through which you manifest.
Give us to know your son. For to know you as you
know man is to know ourselves.
For in knowing this, we are not led into any way
save your way.
And thus we know that this is the God way for us.
God our Father, we see clearly each day that we
may and do forgive every trespass that man has
brought forth into this Kingdom.
Thus we are not tempted to set up man's creations
for your creations.

God our Father,
Again we say, hallowed be the name God.
God our Father.

"YOU HAVE THOUGHT UP
EVERY SPURIOUS TALE"*

YOU HAVE thought up, printed and repeated every spurious tale that can be imagined about the Christ, also the man Jesus, when in reality he has always represented and is today representing the true Christ that is residing, and always has resided, within every individual — representing the God man, the clean, the truly immaculate into full life and form.

This Temple Emmanuel is in as complete form within the first cell as the true form of the tree that the acorn will grow is contained at the very heart cell of the acorn, and the Christ form does come forth perfect from the first cell, as human perversity is held in abeyance.

*Quotation marks used with titles in this section indicate the absence of titles in the manuscripts.

"NOW SPEAK TO THE CHRIST WITHIN"

NOW SPEAK to the Christ within and ask the Christ, Who am I? The answer will always be You are God, for the Christ speaks only absolute Truth. Then take no other view. The Christ is always right.

THE CLOUD-WALKERS OF KASHMIR

THERE IS a Divine science, and that is the science of the mind of all humanity. All of our knowledge is based upon knowledge in which we go from the less general to the greater, or from the general to the particular. Yet it has experience as its basis. In what we call exact science, people easily find the truth, because it appeals to the particular experience of every human being. The scientist does not tell us to believe in anything, but he has certain results that come from his own experiences and reasoning on these experiences. While he asks you to believe in his conclusions, he appeals to some universal experience of humanity. In every exact science there is a universal basis which is common to all humanity, so that we can at once see the truth or fallacy of the conclusions drawn therefrom. Then the question is: has orthodox religion any such basis? Religion as heretofore generally taught nearly all over the world is said to be based on faith and belief, and in most cases consists only of different sets or theories, and that is the reason that we find all of the various religions quarrelling with each other. These theories are, again, based on belief.

One man says that there is a great being sitting above the clouds and governing the entire universe, and he asks me to believe that solely on the theory of his assertion. In the same way I may have my own ideas, which I am asking others to believe; and if they ask a reason, I cannot supply them with any. This is why religion and metaphysical philosophy have a bad name nowadays. Every educated person seems to say: "Oh, these religions are only bundles of theories without any standard to judge them by. Each one preaches his own pet ideas." At the same time, let me tell you that there is a definite basis of universal belief governing all religious beliefs. Going to the basis of them all, we find that they are based on universal experiences.

Thus it is clear that all of the religions of the world have been built upon that universal and adamantine foundation of all of our knowledge—direct experience. Only there is this difference, that in most of these religions, especially in modern times, a peculiar claim is set before us, and that claim is that these experiences are impossible at the present day; they were only possible with a few men, who were the first founders of religions that bore their names. At the present time, these experiences are obsolete, and therefore we have now to take religion on belief. This theory can now be clearly denied. For it can be truthfully said that if there has been one case of experience in this world in any particular branch of knowledge, it absolutely follows that this experience has been possible millions of times before and will be repeated eternally. Uniformity is the rigorous law of nature: what once happened for the good of humanity must and will happen at any time.

There have been more falsehoods in the name of God than in any other cause, and the reason is that people never went to the fountainhead; they were content only to give a menial assent to the customs of their forefathers. They also wanted others to do the same. What right has any person to say that they have a soul unless they say it with the determination that they must know they really have a soul; also that there is a Divine Supreme Power known as God; and unless they definitely know that they are that same Power, and can use it if they will?

It is well known today that any search after a Supreme Being outside of one's self is futile — as it is to believe that an eternal rigmarole of words will find Something outside of themselves. Humanity knows that they must have truth, and they must experience truth for themselves within their heart of hearts. Then they will know that all doubts and discord and darkness vanish. There is a way out of all of this darkness, and that is by knowing that you are the way of God Principle and that you are well established in that Principle, and there is no other way.

In the first place, every science must have its own method of investigation. In the event that you decided to become an astronomer, you would in no way sit down and cry, "Astronomy, astronomy." Without giving any deep thought to the subject, it will never be accomplished. It is the same with any basic science: You will find that certain methods must be followed and that you must give the subject deep thought and full acceptance; that you are fully capable to accomlish your object; and that the accomplishment is right within yourself, and the ability to accomplish is that which you put forth.

Each science must have its own methods. And as we

pursue the truth of Divine Mind within ourselves, we see it is the basis of all Mind action. In fact, this is the truth of all of the sages of all countries, of all ages — people pure and unselfish who had no motive but to do good to the world.

Take up this method and concentrate on the fact that you are pure Divine Mind action and that you are the master of your destiny. Concentrate your thoughts upon it and know that you must observe it as a true science in order to become aware of its full meaning and action. Thus we will come to the basis that we are free, untrammeled souls, fully Divine — that life, instead of a few short years, we fully know is for eternity. The real goal is the ability to concentrate the thoughts on the mind to that point where we know that we are Divine Mind, and at the same time know that we are human beings.

Every human being has the right to ask the reason why, and to have it answered by themselves. In this there is all love, all wisdom, all power, as well as all abundance. This means applying yourself to Perfect Divine Being, which you are.

As you concentrate on these facts, discard all of the rubbish you have been compelling your thoughts and words to store in your subconscious, or subjective, mind. Thus we soon find that there is a Divine purpose throughout the entire universe, and that you are as universal as that Divine purpose. You also know that your body is as pure and sweet as your thoughts make it.

When you take the stand that you know beyond any question of doubt, you also should believe nothing until you find that it is true for yourself. Truth does not need a prop to assist it to stand. The facts of our awakened state require no dreams to prove them. The awakening may be instantaneous, or it may take a long time of constant practice. We are the deciding factor. There is no time but the present. In the event that we decide that time is necessary, we find that the awakening is the present.

You may ask, What is the use of such knowledge? In the first place, knowledge itself is the highest reward of knowledge, and in the second place, there is also utility in it. It will take all of your misery. When, by analyzing our own mind, we come face to face, as it were, with something that is never destroyed, something which is, by its own nature, eternally pure and perfect, we will no more be miserable, no more unhappy. All misery comes from fear, from unsatisfied desire.

There is but one method by which to attain this knowledge: that which is called concentration. The chemist in his laboratory concentrates all of the energies of his mind into one focus and throws them out upon the materials he is analyzing, and so finds out their secrets. The astronomer concentrates all of the energies of his mind into one focus and projects them through his telescope upon the skies; and the stars, the sun, and the moon give up their secrets to him.

How has all of this knowledge in the world been gained but by concentration of the power of the mind? Nature is ready to give up her secrets as we know how to knock, to give her the necessary blow; and the strength and force of the blow comes through concentration. There is no limit to the power of the human mind. The more concentrated it is, the more power is brought to bear on the one point; and that is the secret.

Anything that is secret and mysterious in this system should be at once discarded. The best guide to life is strength. Discard everything that weakens you; have nothing to do with it. All mystery-mongering weakens the human brain. Through it this science has been well-nigh destroyed; but it is one of the grandest of sciences. From the time it was discovered, it was perfectly delineated and formulated and preached in India; and it is a striking fact that the more modern the commentator, the greater the mistakes that are made. The more ancient the writer on it, the more rational he is. Most of the modern writers talk of all sorts of mystery. Thus it fell into the hands of persons that made it a secret, instead of letting the full blaze of daylight and reason fall upon it; and they did so that they might have the power to themselves.

"GOD THE VIBRATORY FORCE"

GOD IS that vibratory Force or Power that all are able to set in motion all about you, which shows you that *you* are able to set it in motion; and every and all things that you can use are for you. God never acts unless man and God act together as one. God is all things, and they are already in existence, but they are quiet, and man is unable to see them, although they are all in the storehouse. The only way to open the door of the storehouse is for man to know that all is God, to act as God and call all things forth. Each and every unit of humanity is capable of accomplishing this as soon as they persist in knowing that they each one are God.

Just go ahead with the complete determination that you can win yourself over as God, and see the windows of heaven open wide and pour out such a blessing that there is not room to receive it all. These windows are the doors of the God storehouse, and once you have opened them, they will never close again. Once they have opened, they will readily open for you. They have in reality never closed except through your own thought. Let go of the thought of the closed doors or windows and you will find them completely open and already pouring out all abundance.

Let go of everything and turn completely to God Spirit, and God Spirit will enter and fill the room and your entire body as well. A great peace will enter your entire body and will never depart again. This is why you become God. Then every inspiration that comes is filled full. Just remember that Elijah held up the cup until it was full or filled full.

There is but the One. It makes no difference how long you have thought separation; you have never accomplished separation. It is only your thoughts that have caused separation to you.

"THERE ARE NO SECRETS IN SUPREME MIND"

THERE ARE no secrets in Supreme Mind, therefore I am Supreme Mind. All there is, is for each and every one to know fully.

I am the Supreme Wisdom, the Supreme Power. All that is in this Great Reservoir of animated thought I am.

As we develop more and accept and recognize this sublime and exhaustless wisdom, we readily draw this wisdom to ourselves and make it a part of ourselves. Humanity fathoms every mystery. Thus all humanity has all-perfecting health and the greatest power to enjoy all that exists. Soon we know that we are all of the Supreme Never-Ending Whole and the Infinite Spirit called God.

God-I-Know that I am the entire never-ending whole of God Purpose. God-I-Know fully that I am the never-ending purpose of God-joy and happiness. How do I know? I have experienced it in its entirety. Why am I so joyous about it? It is because all are capable of being that very thing.

Oh, I see you all so capable; not one need falter or fear. You are every one of you all the mighty God presence. All that is necessary to state is: "God-I-am Supreme Life Immortal. God-I-am Supreme Intelligence Immortal. I am Supreme Wisdom Immortal. I am Supreme Abundance Immortal. I am God, as

well as all others. Every child, every person is God."
There is no guessing here; every person must know
that they as well as all others are Supreme and that
there is nothing missing in the Supreme Energy.

"JESUS SAID . . ."

JESUS SAID, "All ye that are heavy laden, come unto me and I AM will give you rest." He intended that if you would give all of your thoughts of burdens to him, you would be completely released from every burden. He would throw them away, and you could only be burdened as you picked up the thoughts of burdens. This is a simple way of your release from burdens.

Just let go of the thoughts of burdens, and you are completely relieved from them. The conquering Christ gives you perfect freedom. You soar with the birds in perfect freedom. Give the conquering Christ within you the opportunity to free you.

BAIRD T. SPALDING
A EULOGY

DAVID BRUTON

IN THE third volume of *Life and Teaching of the Masters of the Far East* is recorded this happening: a band of raiders were attempting to seize a temple which had long been a meeting place for the Masters. The village below the temple was threatened. At the crucial moment when it seemed inevitable that the raiders would succeed in their plan, this scene occurs:

One member of our party working on the ledge, stopped work and was watching the advancing band. We saw him turn and look through the door leading to the entrance of the center room of the Temple.

Our field glasses were all centered upon the figure of Jesus as He advanced through the door and stepped upon the ledge, walking directly to the brink and standing for a moment with body magnificently poised.

This ledge was about eight hundred feet above where we were concealed and nearly three miles distant. Instantly we realized that He was speaking, and, in another moment, the words came to us clear and distinct. Our associate on the ledge sat down and began taking notes in shorthand, which I did also. Later comparison showed that we heard His words distinctly above the din of the advancing hordes. We were told that He did not raise His voice above His natural well-modulated tones.

159

As Jesus began speaking, a perfect calm came over the entire village and its inhabitants. These are His words, translated into English by Jesus Himself. My most fervent prayer will always be that I shall never forget them, though I live to be ten thousand years.

THE LIGHT

"As I stand alone in Your great silence, God my Father, in the midst of me there blazes a pure light and it fills every atom of my whole being with its great radiance. Life, Love, Strength, Purity, Beauty, Perfection, stand forth in all dominion within me. As I gaze into the very heart of this light, I see another light—liquid, soft, golden-white and radiantly luminous—absorbing, mothering and giving forth the caressing fire of the Greater Light.

"Now I know that I am God and one with God's whole universe. I whisper to God my Father and I am undisturbed."

STILL IN THE SILENCE

"Yet in this complete silence there exists God's Greatest Activity. Again, I am undisturbed and complete silence is all about me. Now the radiance of this light spreads to God's vast universe and everywhere I know there is God's conscious life. Again, I say fearlessly, I am God; I am silent and unafraid.

"I lift the Christ high within me and sing God's praise. In the tones of my music inspiration hums. Louder and louder within me the Great Mother sings of new life. Louder and clearer with each new day, inspiration is lifting my conscious thought until it is attuned to God's rhythm. Again, I lift the Christ high and give close ear that I may hear the glad music. My

keynote is harmony and the theme of my song is God and God seals my song as Truth."

BEHOLD I AM BORN ANEW,
A CHRIST IS HERE

"I am free with the great light of Your Spirit, God my Father, Your seal is placed upon my forehead. I accept.

"I hold your light high, God my Father. Again, I accept."

We are gathered here today to pay homage to a Great Soul, one whose life among us may be more accurately evaluated now that his physical body has come to rest. It is not uncommon for the importance of a life to be accentuated when the form becomes inactive. Edison's life stood out in bold relief after he quit his daily tasks. This was true of Henry Ford, George Eastman and John D. Rockefeller. And certainly, Gandhi's life took on new meaning after his body was stilled.

Friends and admirers of great people often become so engrossed in current events about these personalities that they overlook the immensity of purpose which attends their life.

Now, we pause a few moments in reflection on the almost unbelievable accomplishments and tremendous contributions made in behalf of humanity by our friend Baird T. Spalding. Mr. Spalding was widely known as a research mining engineer as well as a research scientist. Listed among his friends and associated in this field were such names as Edison, Ford,

Guggenheimer, Steinmetz, Burbank and the explorer Andersen. His activities in mining and research science were widespread, extending from Alaska, the United States, South America, Australia and India.

Besides his life in science and mining, Mr. Spalding, in writing the four volumes of *Life and Teaching of the Masters of the Far East*, commanded worldwide attention. Scarcely any name of prominence during the past 75 years has failed to come into contact with him. As in science and mining, his friends in philosophic and metaphysical work included the most famous of our time—Claude Bragdon, Kahlil Gibran, Paul Brunton, Bruce Barton, Krishnamurti, Annie Besant, Mme. Blavatsky and metaphysical leaders throughout the world. His wide list of friends encircled the globe.

Baird Spalding was a simple man with simple living habits. His most outstanding character trait was kindness. His whole nature was extremely gentle. He had a deep affection for everyone he knew. He would go a thousand miles to do a favor for a friend. His life was enriched by almost constant travel. His scope of experience and memory were both phenomenal. He was equally conversant with Alaska, Canada, United States, Mexico, South America, Australia, Africa, India, China, Europe and the Orient as he was with Los Angeles. In talking with him, the world seemed terribly small.

Although Baird Spalding had a multitude of friends and acquaintances all over the world, there were few people who knew him well enough to penetrate more than his superficial activities. And fewer still ever caught a glimpse of the cosmic significance of his being here. His true life-mission lay in his writing the four volumes of *Life and Teaching of the Masters of the Far East*. It is difficult to realize, as yet, the far-reaching effect of his work. But let us consider what this man has actually done.

Before the release of his books, the world had plodded along in the same spiritual trends for centuries. While religions taught the resurrection of Jesus and that He continued to live, His life as a direct contact with humanity had, in most instances, become vague and unrealistic. The word *Master* carried with it an imaginary, superhuman state of Divinity that was awesome and apart from the attainment of ordinary human beings. The miracles of Jesus were tabulated as something which could occur at that period of history, and by Him alone, but were not linked with possibilities of modern times, although Jesus taught "Greater things than these shall ye do."

Thirty years ago, when the account of Mr. Spalding's experience with Jesus and the Masters of the Far East came to light, a New Age of spiritual understanding was born. The release of his first book ushered in the New Age spiritual concept just as definitely as the dropping of the atom bomb on Hiroshima marked the beginning of the atomic age. Herein lies the cosmic destiny of Baird T. Spalding; and it is my firm conviction that in the past 30 years, Baird T. Spalding — and he alone — has contributed more to the enlightenment of mankind than any other individual or organized group, or even the sum total of individuals and organized groups have done in the past two hundred years.

More than one million copies of his books are in circulation. They have been translated into Danish, Italian, French and German. The largest book sales, at present, are in Johannesburg, South Africa, and Australia. Large orders pour in from England, Canada and South America — not to mention a constant flow of orders from every state in the union.

The influence of Baird Spalding's work will live in the New Age. It has paved the way for all teachers who present the teaching of a Master. From this point, it remains the responsibility of us who are now here to carry on. Mr. Spalding fulfilled his cosmic duty, and that duty was fulfilled as only he could have done it.

At this time, I should like to introduce to you the man who has been a vital factor in assisting Mr. Spalding carry out his tremendous work. Douglas K. DeVorss was not only Mr. Spalding's partner but his business manager and personal representative for the past 20 years. It is through their combined efforts that Mr. Spalding's work will be carried on in the future. I present to you Douglas K. DeVorss.*

* * *

*See *Life and Teaching of the Masters of the Far East*, vol. 5, pp. 9-15.

In closing, I would like to pronounce this Benediction. One of Mr. Spalding's favorite topics of conversation was the Light that lighteth every man that cometh into the world. And, now as we close, let us know:

There is a Light that lighteth every man that cometh into the world. That Light is Eternal, All-Powerful and Imperishable. Only that which is subject to birth is subject to death. The Light is the extension of God into man. It is not born nor can it die.

We wish you Godspeed, Baird Spalding, in your greater expansion of life.

BAIRD T. SPALDING

A REMINISCENCE

LOIS BINFORD PROCTOR

MY FRIEND the late Dr. Neva Dell Hunter knew Baird very well and gave me some fascinating information.

Baird was actually Baird Spalding III. His father was Baird Spalding II, and his grandfather, to whom he was very close, was Baird Spalding the first! Baird III always spoke of him as "Grandpappy," and it seems he really had been born in India.

Dr. Hunter, at that time, was constantly on lecture tours, traveling all over the country. While in the same town one time, Baird contacted her and came over to the house where she was staying.

"Neva Dell," he said excitedly, "come out and see my new car and come with me to the garage. I have to get an oil change and checkup." So she went with him and they had a nice visit until the mechanic came over with a puzzled expression on his face.

"Mr. Spalding," he began, "this is a new car. You've only had it a month, and yet your speedometer reading is over 5000 miles. How could you possibly have driven that much in a month?"

Baird just laughed it off. "I don't know — I just like to drive, I guess."

On the way home, Neva Dell said, "All right, Baird: how did you put all those miles on this car?"

Baird grinned and said, "Well, I've been taking a lot of long trips lately, and I always drive at night. I just get in the car and say, 'O.K., Grandpappy; you take over,' and I go to sleep! Grandpappy drives like the wind," he added.

Neva Dell was aghast. "You mean you actually go to sleep at the wheel and Grandpappy does the driving?"

"Sure," he answered; "we're very close, you know. We talk all the time."

Baird Spalding seemed to have no sense of time or distance. He lived, or at least thought, in another dimension. One time, Dr. Hunter was giving a talk at Santa Barbara, and Baird came to the lecture. Afterwards he came up and asked her to go out for a cup of coffee. She agreed, and they started driving out of town. They drove and drove, and she wondered just where they were going for that "cup of coffee" and finally asked him. (Grandpappy wasn't driving that time.) He said casually, "Oh, just up the road a ways. I want you to meet a friend of mine."

They kept driving until nearly 1:00 A.M., when they came to San Luis Obispo and drove up to a house. Baird knocked on the door and then threw small pebbles at the upstairs window. A sleepy voice called out, "Who is it?"

"It's Baird Spalding," he replied, "and I've brought a friend for a cup of coffee!"

A woman came down in her robe and let them in and then cheerfully prepared the coffee while Baird chatted cozily. She offered to get beds ready for them but he said, "Well, just for Neva Dell; I'm not stay-ing. I'm on my way to San Francisco."

Neva Dell was flabbergasted. "Well, what am I sup-posed to do?" she gasped. "How will I get back to Santa Barbara?"

"Don't worry," he smiled, "it's all been arranged. You'll find out in the morning. Good night, and thanks for the coffee." And he was off!

The next morning, while they were having break-fast, a friend of her hostess stopped by. "This is a quick hello," he said. "I don't know why I stopped; I'm on my way to Los Angeles, but something kept nudging me to stop and see you. Are you all right?"

The woman told him she was fine but would he please take her guest, Dr. Hunter, with him and drop her off in Santa Barbara? He said he'd be delighted to have the company, and away they went.

When Dr. Hunter was in New York City, she always stayed at the Great Northern Hotel. One afternoon, Baird Spalding came over for a visit and he casually mentioned that he had to be in Canada that evening as he was lecturing in Montreal at the Women's Club.

They had a fascinating conversation but it was almost 5 o'clock and he hadn't made a move to leave. "What time is your lecture?" Neva Dell asked. "Shouldn't you be leaving?"

"Oh no," Baird replied. "It's not until 7:30, and I have plenty of time."

So they continued talking until Baird finally said goodbye and left. By that time it was close to 6:00 P.M., and Dr. Hunter was very nervous. He would hardly have time to get ready and go to the airport, much less Montreal! She waited until nearly 7:30 and then put in a call to the Women's Club in Montreal.

"Please tell me," she said, "has Baird Spalding arrived yet?"

The woman who answered said, "Why, he's walking up on the platform right now."

It was Dr. Hunter's belief, and mine, that Baird Spalding I (Grandpappy) had taken over the body of Baird Spalding III, almost like a "walk-in," as we say today. But it was not a total takeover. Baird Spalding III was still in the body too; but Grandpappy could walk in and out as necessary, and apparently Baird never really knew "who" he was at any given time.

I would assume that this arrangement had been agreed upon on the Inner Planes before Baird Spalding III was born. This would explain the seeming discrepancies in some of the statements that were made, as well as other matters.

FROM THE "LOST"
SPALDING ARCHIVES

Baird T. Spalding

LIFE AND TEACHING OF THE MASTERS OF THE FAR EAST

CALIFORNIA PRESS
Publishers
BROADWAY AND SANSOME STREETS
SAN FRANCISCO, CALIFORNIA

Title page of Volume 1, first edition (1924). Note the absence of Spalding's name, which was given on the cover.

Under personal management of Douglas K. DeVorss

BAIRD T. SPALDING

Author, THE LIFE AND TEACHING OF THE MASTERS OF THE FAR EAST

will make the following public appearances in your city to meet you personally, autograph his new book, VOLUME THREE, and answer your questions regarding the teachings of the Masters.

... In New York ...

PUBLIC LECTURES
THURSDAY, SEPTEMBER 12, 1935—2:30 P. M.
THURSDAY, SEPTEMBER 12, 1935—8:00 P. M.
CHURCH OF THE TRUTH, 521 FIFTH AVE., Rm. 728
FRIDAY, SEPTEMBER 13, 1935—8:00 P. M.
UNIVERSAL TRUTH CENTRE SCHOOL, 360 W. 125th St.

FOR AUTOGRAPHING
FRIDAY, SEPTEMBER 13, 1935—11:00 A. M.
R. H. MACY & CO., Inc., BROADWAY at 34th

You and your friends are cordially invited to attend.
Read carefully other particulars.

The New York City portion of Spalding's and DeVorss' 1-month, 10-state (+ D.C. & Toronto), 20-city lecture and book-signing barnstorm immediately prior to the India Tour (4 Oct. 1935).

Portion of the India Tour group, Oct. 4, 1935, immediately before embarkation from San Francisco on the S. S. President Hoover. Baird Spalding is the sixth figure from the right. Douglas De Vorss, the fifth from left.

DEAUVILLE POOL
S. S. PRESIDENT HOOVER
Super Express

WRITING ROOM
(Special Class)
S. S. PRESIDENT HOOVER
Super Express

WRITING ROOM
S. S. PRESIDENT HOOVER
Super Express

SMOKING ROOM
S S PRESIDENT HOOVER
Super Express

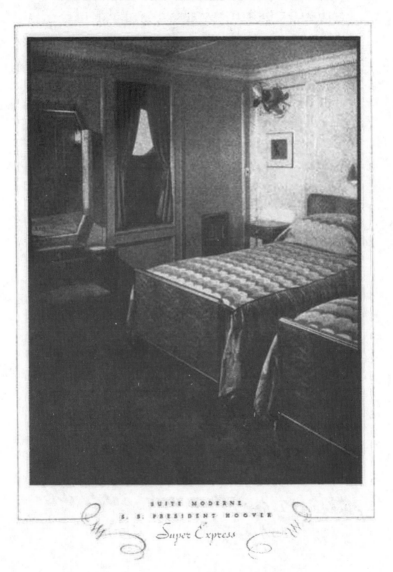

SUITE MODERNE
S. S. PRESIDENT HOOVER
Super Express

DOLLAR STEAMSHIP LINES

ROUND THE WORLD
ORIENT AND PACIFIC

Dear Mr. DeVorss —
Everything Ok by us —
hope its same by you.
Hot & Humid in Manila;
Have made some
wonderfull contacts —
every thing seems to be
just right — all in Divine
Order.

The daily meetings are
Wonderfull; the Secretary
is good but you don't
get near all of it in
these reports — especially the
Spirit of it;

Letter from John A. Balsley, M.D., India Tour correspondent, to Douglas DeVorss. Although it bears no date, a marking indicates that it was received in Los Angeles on Nov. 21, 1935.

184

Grace is doing fine. Her splints come off tomorrow — Results perfect. Dr. Hand is snapping out of it, at last, and all the rest are app + at the totals 3X daily.

8 of us go directly to Calcutta, the others go to Bombay + the longer way round — sight seeing —

Guess that is about all the news for this time, —

God bless you in the great work — Sincerely

J. Balsley

Please phone Mr. B. every thing is O.K.

BRITISH INDIA STEAM NAVIGATION Co. Ltd.

S.S.

Nov. 7 – 35.

Mr. Douglas De Voras.
Trinity Bldg.
Grand Ave. & 9 St.
Los Angeles Calif.
Dear Mr. DeVorss.

We are on this boat nearing Rangoon and only about two days from Calcutta and the end of our boat journey.

This has been a most enjoyable trip more particularly as we have not had a storm during

Letter from Baird Spalding to Douglas DeVorss, "two days from Calcutta," Nov. 7, 1935.

the whole time from the day we left San Francisco.

At Rangoon we will have mailed you sixteen lessons, and will resume them as soon as possible after reaching Calcutta.

We will probably be located in Calcutta for some time, as we will attempt to establish head-quarters there. You will hear from us often after this.

Regards to all
Baird T. Spalding

Pages from Baird Spalding's guidebook.

The First Impression

A BIRDS-EYE VIEW OF CALCUTTA.

Photograph by Bourne & Shepherd, Calcutta.

THE JAIN TEMPLE.

Photograph by Johnston & Hoffmann, Calcutta.

HOWRAH STATION.

Photograph by Bourne & Shepherd, Calcutta.

SS. PRESIDENT HOOVER
DOLLAR STEAM SHIP LINES

Dec, 1st 1935

Dear Douglas DeVoss –

Thanks a lot for th first monthly remittance – it was a life saver.

No word of any kind from you since Oct 4th – except through Mr, Balsley, How come?

Send us a letter – soon – full of news – from Home sweet Home. Did you get th lessons? 16 of them? We sent them, type written, all OK.

Letter from Dr. Balsley to Douglas DeVorss, Dec. 1, 1935. The second page offers a glowing account of Spalding's reunion with people at Calcutta University and figures prominently in a DeVorss & Co. promotional piece of Dec. 26th (see p. 197).

B. T. S. now carrying on with his Research work. In Calcutta University we have met some of his former teachers – Prof's. Ghose – Physics Dept. Jenis Bose, Mag, Roy, Das, etc of transcendental Physics, Physiology, Chemistry, Metaphysics, Philosophy. And the Science College – we sat in the hall he used to occupy along side of Eddington – under the great Laters – which gives one a very strange and beautiful experience – a feeling of wonder, because of the marvelous acoustics! almost

a whispering gallery - Yet, it has never been
reproduced even by the best Architects
with copying instruments - there is
something there that cannot be
reproduced. Bose & Ghose & Ray &
Das are Wonderful! So is Neog -
They have something over here
that is real thing - They know
the Past by what is cause
becomes effect & vice versa.

will send you more later.
Send Grace another Hundred.
we need it for B.T.S. You
have signed contracts. —regardless
of what any one writes. carry
out the Contracts. Grace is the
one responcible to you — Send
it to no one else,

Merry Christmas &
a Happy New Year —

Sincerely Dr. Balsley

God bless You for the Great Work,

FLASH!   FLASH!   FLASH!

TO FRIENDS AND STUDENTS OF THE BAIRD T. SPALDING INDIA TOUR
LESSONS - - -

We have just received from Dr. John A. Balsley,
eminent physician of Los Angeles and a member of the Spalding
Round the World Tour, a Special Delivery Air Mail letter from
Calcutta, India, and we are pleased to quote extracts from
this letter for your information.

December 2, 1935

"Baird T. Spalding is now carrying on with his
research work in Calcutta University. We have met some of
his former teachers, Professors Ghose, Physics Department,
Jessie Bose, Nag, Roy, Das, etc., of Transcendental Physics,
Physiology, Chemistry, Metaphysics and Philosophy, all of
the Science College. We sat in the seat he used to occupy
along side of Eddington, under the great Lotus, which gives
one a very strange and beautiful experience--a feeling of
wonder because of the marvelous acoustics--almost a whispering gallery. Yet it has never been reproduced even by the
best architects with copied measurements. There is something there that cannot be reproduced. Bose and Ghose and
Roy and Das are wonderful! So is Nag.

They have something over here that is the real
thing. They know the Great Law! The Law by which cause
becomes effect, and vice versa. Will send you more later."

(Signed)   John A. Balsley

Now that these reports are beginning to reach
us direct from India, we hope to have even more startling
experiences to relate.

DeVORSS & CO.
843 S. Grand,
Los Angeles

December 26, 1935

THE LIFE OF THE MASTERS OF THE FAR EAST

The Purpose and Nature

of the

INDIA TOUR LESSONS

By Baird T. Spalding*

The purpose of these Lessons is to emphasize the application of the Christ teaching and principle in human life. The course of Lessons will take in the full scope of the vision of the Masters.

Wherever there is a flare of general interest in any personality or his achievement there is a flame of spiritual truth accompanying it. No other person in modern times has created such a flare of general interest as has Baird T. Spalding. No other has seemed to sense the flame of spiritual inspiration now sweeping the world, as has he. The nature of the man, the manner in which his message has been presented and the message, all bear living testimony to the vitality of his message. No one can afford to overlook the tremendous opportunity afforded by this new presentation of an age-old message. Every age demands its own revelations of Truth. Though Truth is the same in all ages, yet as it is reborn in each age it comes with the flame of inspiration and is received with a corresponding flame of enthusiasm springing from hearts ready to be born into full realization of the glory that awaits them; the new revelation is but the atmosphere into which they are born again. Why wait for rebirth in another life when the birth into true existence is the tangible possibility awaiting each individual in this very day?

These Lessons of Mr. Spalding's are deep and vital yet grandly simple, speaking the language of the soul of all men. They voice what every man longs to voice and express in his own life. "You can overlook it for eternity if you want to," says Mr. Spalding. "still, the moment you return to it you yourself will return to perfect condition and this human body gets the result of that determination." He further says, "It only takes one Master Mind to create peace, but there are millions today thinking along that line." It is impossible to foresee the far reaching effect that sincere groups of people working along together may have upon determining the progress of the present generation. It is time that we go to work in earnest, dig deep into the true facts of life and with like determination live these facts collectively and individually. It is our sacred duty to ourselves and our civilization to "have a mind to work." Ours is a sacred privilege to take our places in the Divine Scheme of things, lay hard hold this truly Christ message and work the works of Him who sent us into being.

EDITOR'S NOTE: The India Tour Lessons became Vol. 4 of *Life & Teaching*. There is now no separate Teacher's Edition, nor do we know of any current study groups.

TEACHING OF THE MASTERS OF THE FAR EAST

Special Information

Regarding the New

BAIRD T. SPALDING[*]

INDIA TOUR LESSONS

The large number of subscriptions and inquiries which have flooded our office since the announcement of the INDIA TOUR LESSONS has made it impossible for Mr. Spalding or Mr. DeVorss to answer personally each inquiry. Your interest in these Lessons is none the less appreciated.

Mr. Spalding and a group of eighteen students sailed from San Francisco October 4, 1935, on the Dollar Liner, President Hoover, arriving in Calcutta, India, November 14, 1935. Accompanying the group is a special correspondent from DeVorss & Co. who is reporting the Lessons given the group by Mr. Spalding. These reports are being sent direct to DeVorss & Co. (Mr. Spalding's publishers), and the first group of Lessons given on board ship en route have been received. Lesson One starts on or about December 1, 1935, and the series runs for 15 weeks at least and perhaps thirty weeks.

TEACHER'S EDITION

In a hundred or more cities teachers and leaders are being appointed to conduct weekly classes for the purpose of reading and studying together the instruction in the BAIRD T. SPALDING INDIA TOUR LESSONS. The leader of each group receives each week a special Teacher's Edition which contains, in addition to the regular Lesson, a specific course of study for the Lesson. An order of meeting is presented with definite instructions on what points should be brought out most effectively. Ideas for opening and closing and conducting meetings are given so that all groups may be conducted in keeping with the spirit of Mr. Spalding's writings.

If you wish to organize a class in your community, write to us now giving us your qualifications and experience as a teacher, stating what courses of study in metaphysics you have followed and what books you have used.

The price of the Teacher's Edition is $1.00 per week, payable in advance each week or for as many weeks as desired. The purchase of the Teacher's Edition entitles the purchaser to order Students' Editions for resale at twenty-five cents (25¢) per copy, a commission being paid the subscriber on all such editions purchased. All enrollments for Teachers' Editions must be directed to DeVorss & Co., accompanied by at least $1.00. $12.50 in advance pays for the first fifteen Lessons.

*See note at foot of preceding page.

Under Personal Management of
Mr. Douglas K. DeVorss

BAIRD T. SPALDING

World Traveler, Scientist and Author,

LIFE AND TEACHING OF THE MASTERS OF THE FAR EAST

(Volumes 1, 2, 3 & 4)

Will make the following public appearances to meet you personally, autograph his latest book, VOLUME FOUR, and answer your questions regarding the Masters . . . . .

Tuesday evening at 8 P.M. - September 18, 1951

Wednesday evening at 8 P.M. - September 19, 1951

Thursday evening at 8 P.M. - September 20, 1951

WOMAN'S CLUB AUDITORIUM

Sierra at Seville, FONTANA, CALIFORNIA

(One-half mile south of Highway 66 on Sierra Avenue)

(Fontana is 48 miles east of Los Angeles)

COME EARLY

You and your friends are cordially invited to attend.

(Free Will Offering)

Comments about Mr. Spalding's Lectures

"I have never heard a more practical, living, simple explanation of the basic principles — God — than that given by Mr. Spalding in his lectures. You feel and know that daily living is easily perfect by reason of the perfection of the Christ within you. Anyone hearing Mr. Spalding will realize the simplicity of life as he himself exemplifies it in his case of expression of many vital truths spoken through him when he is on the platform." — E. E. P., Los Angeles

A RARE OPPORTUNITY TO HEAR AND MEET THIS FAMOUS AUTHOR

Do you know the origin of the flying saucers, and the principle of their operation?	DO YOU KNOW OF ANYONE OTHER THAN THE MASTERS WHO HAVE ATTAINED COMPLETE MASTERY OVER OLD AGE AND DEATH.
What complexion, hair coloring is the man Jesus?	Is the Name of Jesus as powerful as the Name of God?
1. Were the masters fully dressed or partly dressed when they walked across the river? 2. How did they get their clothes across the river to where they were? 3. Did you see Etheric bodies or were they built up physical flesh bodies? (over)	Is cremation the preferred way of disposing of a dead body?
Please explain what happened to make people think they saw Jesus crucified.	Will you give more details about how the camera pictured Jesus? — light conditions type of film, etc.

Handwritten questions sent up to Spalding after the lectures delivered at Fontana.

Doctor, The Rt. Honorable COUNTESS OF MAYO F.R.G.S.
President
Truth in Action · Edinburgh, Scotland
Phychological Research Society · Manchester, England
Council of Truth Centers · Manchester, England
Former Group President
International New Thought Alliance · United Kingdom
Lectures
Edinburgh · San Francisco
Saturdays and Sundays, 8 p. m. · Thursdays 8 p m
Inner Silent Union Healing
Thursdays 8 p. m. · Mondays 2 and 8 p. m.
Free Consultations after Lectures for 1 Hour
Private by appointment

140 PRINCES STREET

EDINBURGH SCOTLAND

TELEPHONES 20420· 26102

AND

SAN FRANCISCO 17, CALIFORNIA

U. S. A.

TELEPHONE UN. 1-4988

Cordova Hotel.   Post Street,
March 6th O. R. 3. 4321
Ex. 301.

My dear Mr Spalding,

If you could only know what your books have done for me and many of my friends, to whom I have recommended your books, you would indeed reply'My dear'also as I address you! They have given me so much to which to strive to attain, and stimulated me to wonderful heights.

I have been trying to find you in the phone book, Library and even through the County Council tax office'. I should so very much like to meet you.

I enclose a little experience of my trip of getting here, and perhaps when you have read it you will see that I am very genuine and will make an appointment with me. I have to send this to your published of your 4th book, which I am delighted you see that you are continuing in your writing.

I AM giving you Countless Blessings,

Noël Mayo

I was on the air the AM such fun.

Spalding received innumerable letters from devoted readers, including—in this case—a countess. A pencil'd date shows March 6, 1953.

CLASSES
CONSULTATIONS
EAST 8784

PASTOR OF
DAYTON NEW THOUGHT TEMPLE
24 GRAFTON AVENUE
DAYTON, OHIO

REV. SHIRLEY BELL HASTINGS

STUDIO -- LIBRARY -- BOOK SHOP

3152 LINWOOD ROAD
CINCINNATI 8, OHIO

Mar, 3, 1952

Dear Mr Spalding:-

I am Shirley Bell Hastings. A few
years ago you spoke at the Hotel Alms, Cincinnati
Ohio and then went with me to my Church, The
Dayton New Thought Temple to speak. Remember,
you stayed at my home 3152 Linwood Road, Cincinnati
Ohio.

We are eager to have you come to Dayton
as they all love you there. Our church has grown
and you would enjoy it.

Have tried several times to contact you,
but like the rest of the world we just didn't know
where you were, but we have been hearing the
rumbles from the West that you are back in harness
again. Am sending this letter in care of De Vorss
Publishing Company, will you please give me
information as to the date, if and when you could
come and speak to us at my Church, The Dayton New

TEACHING OF THE MASTERS OF THE FAR EAST

CLASSES
CONSULTATIONS
EAST 5794

PASTOR OF
DAYTON NEW THOUGHT TEMPLE
24 GRAFTON AVENUE
DAYTON, OHIO

REV. SHIRLEY BELL HASTINGS
STUDIO -- LIBRARY -- BOOK SHOP
3152 LINWOOD ROAD
CINCINNATI 8, OHIO

Thought Temple, 24 Grafton Ave, Dayton, Ohio.

I consider myself one of your good friends, and you one of my precious friends. Am looking forward with pleasure to seeing you.

We will comply with any request you make. Please try to get some word back to us as we are so eager to have you come.

Your friend, Dr. A. L. Mc Gowan passed on three or four years ago. You may have known of his passing, but I am mentioning it.

Letters are such cold things some how but we feel so warm toward you. Your last message given into our group "I Am God" still rings, I know you have much more to put into our consciousness.

With all my love and the love of my people and greetings from my husband.

Believe me

Friend -

Shirley Bell Hastings.

Spalding lived almost reclusively yet had devoted friends almost everywhere. This letter is one of many such.

G. Elink Schuurman

Los Pat. May 4, 1953.

Mr. Baird T. Spalding,
c/o Messrs. DeVorss & Co., Publishers,
843 South Grand Avenue,
Los Angeles, California.

Dear Mr. Spalding:

Seeing that I entirely lack the makings of an author or
someone accustomed to write I do not possess that enviable
quality of being able to accurately translate my innermost
thoughts and feelings into words. Nevertheless, I take the
liberty of addressing these lines to you in the hope that
you will be able to read between the lines, and feel my
deep appreciation for the many hours of reading pleasure
which your book "Life and Teaching of the Masters of the
Far East" has afforded me. Truly a masterpiece, a poem
which enchants the soul! Thank you so much for what you
have given me; not now, or ever, could I repay you for
that added light which your most revealing book has cast
upon my path.

I avail myself of this opportunity to inform you that
my wife and I are planning to visit Tibet sometime later
this year, that is to say .... if conditions permit us to
do so. The sole purpose of our trip is to search for learning, always more learning - healthy clean food for the soul!
Just imagine the possibility of ever meeting your friends
there, Jast, Emil, the beautiful Lady, not to speak of the
Master Jesus!! After reading your book these people have
also become my friends.

Our Gurudeva, Mrs. Violette V. Daschkoff, is going
with us - first to Shigatze, then .... I do not know, but
let us say to there where God's guiding hand will bring us.

Dear Brother, fare ye well! With very best wishes for
your personal well-being, and for Peace Profound, I am,

Most sincerely yours,

P.O. Box 7033,
São Paulo, Brazil.

This is typical of the more colorful kind of correspondence
that Spalding received.

St. Louis, Mo.
21 July 1950

Mr. Baird T. Spalding
De Vorss Publishers
843 South Grand Avenue
Los Angeles 14, California

Dear Mr. Spalding:

As you are the Author of "Life and Teaching of
the Masters of the Far East," I am writing to you as there are so
many, many things I would like to know more about, but the most
important to me is to be healed of double curvature of the spine
and a dislocated left hip, abnormal stomach, hips, etc.

I have been interested in Christian Science since
1918, and have been studying all these years, but so far have not
attained the understanding to be free of the belief of deformity.
I have received wonderful help from Christian Science, and I cannot
express in words how grateful I really am for it.

Mr. Spalding you state in your book "Our Chief
said, "Please be silent. Our dear Master, Jesus, is speaking," and
that he was in the room shaking hands and saying, "I love them with
a love that is unspeakable, "I have not withdrawn from them," etc.
Now if there is someone who has risen so high in consciousness as
to be able to talk, shake hands, etc., with Jesus, will you please
ask that one the next time he talks with Jesus to please ask him
to cure me of deformity, etc., and give me a higher spiritual understanding of the Truth.

I know Jesus heals instantly, and I expect to be
free instantly of the claim and be perfect.

I want to express my gratitude to you Mr. Spalding
for seeing that this letter reaches the proper channel. Many, many
thanks for your kindness. You will do that for me, won't you please
Mr. Spalding?

A self addressed stamped envelope is enclosed for
your convenience.

I am anxiously awaiting a reply.

Yours sincerely,

Emma F. Frevert

Miss Emma F. Frevert
2134 E. John Avenue
St. Louis 7, Missouri

Spalding also received many letters of petition like this one.

* * *

The great interest in, and popularity of, *Life and Teaching of the Masters of the Far East* gave rise to the organization of classes from coast to coast teaching from the books. To facilitiate this activity, *Mind Magazine* published a suggested ORDER OF MEETINGS.

The following pages give the proposed Order and record Baird Spalding's reaction to one such activity as reported to him. Douglas DeVorss then smooths matters over.

(Note that Spalding is addressed by his friend as "Bill." His own use of "Dug" for "Doug" was a facetious mannerism.)

* * *

ORDER OF MEETINGS

(Offerings should be made at the door of classroom when the student enters. Any preliminaries, such as announcements, songs—if they are used—et cetera, should precede the devotional and study period. These out of the way, proceed by reading the following from Volume III, Page 40, Life and Teaching of the Masters of the Far East. *Entire class should be in meditation and a period of silence should follow for at least a half minute after each section of the paragraph as indicated. This time may be increased as the ability of the entire class becomes such that they can properly meditate for a longer period.)*

* * *

"Yet in this complete silence there exists God's greatest activity. Again I am undisturbed, and complete silence is all about me."

PAUSE

"Now the radiance of this light spreads to God's vast universe, and everywhere I know there is God's constant life. Again I say, fearlessly, I am God; I am silent and unafraid."

PAUSE

"I lift the Christ high within me and sing God's praise. In the tones of my music inspiration hums. Louder and louder within me the Great Mother sings of new life. Louder and clearer with each new day, inspiration is lifting my conscious thought until it is attuned to God's rhythm."

PAUSE

"Again I lift the Christ high and give close ear that I may hear the glad music. My keynote is harmony, and the theme of my song is God, and God seals my song as TRUTH."

PAUSE

(Proceed with the lesson at this point.)

(After the lesson, ask the class to stand for closing meditation, which they should learn to repeat in unison.)

"I am free with the great light of YOUR SPIRIT, God, my Father. Your seal is placed upon my forehead; I accept."

PAUSE

AMEN!

(Class to be dismissed without further word, each going in silence and keeping his consciousness high and as sacredly as the most earnest might keep his vows before men.)

YOU ARE INVITED TO ATTEND THE SPECIAL CLASSES ON . . . .

LIFE AND TEACHING OF THE MASTERS OF THE FAR EAST

by Baird T. Spalding

To be Conducted by ARTHUR W. SMITH, D.D., Special Representative

Starting Tuesday evening, August 8, 1950 at 8 o'clock.

This series of lessons is being given at the request of many Truth students and will continue every Tuesday evening for fifteen weeks.

Love offering, one dollar per lesson. Tell your friends.

Meetings will be held at:

715 Esplanade
Redondo Beach, California
Telephone Frontier 43127

UNDER THE AUSPICES OF
THE HOLY SCIENCE BROTHERHOOD

EDWARD K. PLEMING, C.S.
4817 VISTA STREET
LONG BEACH 3, CALIFORNIA

August 9, 1950

Dear Bill:

Hello and best wishes from us all. I phoned Mrs. Welsh yesterday and told her of the classes being held at Redondo Beach on your books by Arthur W. Smith, as per enclosed card which was mailed to our friends, the Mitchells. Mrs. Welsh knew nothing about these meetings and I was inclined to think that perhaps you did not. Laura and I attended last night. They are being held in a lovely, well furnished home, overlooking the ocean. As we entered, oriental music was being softly played on a beautiful console phonograph, amid much incense. About twenty-six were present. Shortly after eight, Mr Smith came into the large sitting room. He seemed to be around forty years of age; very handsome, very gracious. After greeting us, he sat down at a small table and invited us to enter into meditation with him. What he asked that we repeat was sensible and well chosen. Then he took up volume four of your books and told us how you had dealt more with phenomena than the cause of that phenomena. He said that he had studied with the Masters for fifteen years and was well qualified to acquaint us with that cause. His first lesson was on Chapter 1. He would read a paragraph and then comment thereon. He would also invite those present to read; a few did, but it seemed to me with little true understanding. He deplored war and stressed peace. It almost seemed he favored peace at any cost. One gentleman said something to the effect that to work for peace as he presented it, we would have to oppose our present war efforts in Korea; would have to desist from opposing aggression, and yet he felt that Italy should have been stopped in their Ethiopian campaig. All present did not seem to follow him. Somehow or other, I could not feel certain. While he spoke of spirituality, it seemed very mortal.

P.S. Laura felt so disturbed about the meeting that she felt that possibly the F.B.I. should be notified.

Laura seemed to stop him pretty muchly by asking if we should take no steps towards resisting the assault of a maddog. He said he felt we were confronted by no mad dog. Yes, and no. Laura and I could not help but wonder. It seemed he regarded Mr. DeVorss highly, but I could not be sure you were held in such esteem. Maybe I was over critical. Before the meeting was finished, I asked: "Does Mr. Spalding know of these meetings and do they have his approval?" "Yes, definitely", he replied. He then said that you had been in Los Angeles a week ago Monday, which would be July 31; that you were now in San Francisco and that he thought you would be present at one of the meetings within two weeks. Knowing you as we do, somehow or other, the meeting just didn't seem to smack of you. At the close of the meeting, he announced that due to cir- cumstances beyond his control and that of the people in whose home they were meeting, their next meeting would be held on Monday evening at eight, at their home in Long Beach at 3018 East First Street. All of your books were on sale at the meeting and Mr. Smith said that he hoped that all would have a copy of Volume Four by the next meeting.

We hope we were wrong in thinking that we smelled a rat. These are days when subversive activities would hide behind the robes of Christ. So we thought that at least you should know. I urged Mrs. Welsh to attend the next meeting here in Long Beach. She felt so certain that you did not know of the meetings that you might attempt to be present if you could make it. I don't believe Laura or I shall attend again.

We think of you often, appreciate you much, and hope to see you soon.

Love from us all,

Ed

FIFTY MODERN STEAM-HEATED ROOMS

COFFEE SHOP   BARBER SHOP

Hotel Enders

J. M. FRASER, Owner

SODA SPRINGS, IDAHO
ON HIGHWAY 30 N   Aug. 18,50.

Dear Dug:

I am in receipt of a letter from Mr. Pleming which I am enclos-
ing as it speaks for itself. I do not know this Mr. Smith or
have I given him any authority to represent me in any way or to
give classes under my name. Therefore I wish you would ask him
to stop this as it may lead to trouble.

Will you also mail me two paper bound Life and Teachings vol.11,
111. Kindly mail them to Soda Springs, Idaho c/o Enders Hotel.

My work at this place will keep me here for about two weeks yet,
then I expect to return to Los Angeles and finish the book as I
have received the information that I have been waiting for, and
I will be able to finish the shortly after my return.

             Thanking you I am
             Sincerely yours,

                    B. T. Spalding.

World renowned Soda Springs Geyser located just back of hotel. Carbon-dioxide gas pressure forces water 125 to 175 feet high.
Soda Springs is in the center of the world's largest deposit of phosphate.

214

843 South Grand Avenue   TUcker
Los Angeles 14, California   7092

August 21, 1950

Mr. Baird T. Spalding
Hotel Enders
Soda Springs, Idaho

Dear Baird:

Thanks for your letter and order. We have
shipped to you today the books you asked for.

I can explain who Rev. Arthur W. Smith is. He
is a new minister who has been deeply interested
in your writings for some time. At the request
of several of his followers he started a class
using LIFE AND TEACHING OF THE MASTERS OF THE
FAR EAST as textbooks, etc.

I have known Rev. Smith for several years. He
was in charge of the Boston Self Realization
work founded by Yogananda and after fifteen years
at that work has started his own ministry.

Rev. Smith asked for permission to use the books
in his class work and we thought it was a good
idea as we have many persons asking where they
can study the books. He has been almost impatient
with me because I have been unable to arrange an
appointment for him to meet you but during July
you were away so much of the time it was not
possible to get the two of you together. I advised
him that it was all right to teach the books and
as soon as you returned we would do our best to
arrange for him to meet you personally.

I understand that at the first meeting two individuals
refused to give their names at the registration table
and that some party tried to embarrass him with tricky
questions such as we had from the M.I.T. boys in Boston.
Remember?
We have several new classes around over the country who
are using the books for fall classes just as they have
been for the last twenty years.
I appreciate your thoughtfulness in writing me as you did.

With every good wish,

c::Edward K. Fleming

Tularosa New Mexico
Sept 17 1952
P.O. Box 1460

Mr. John Lonn
2535 Third Aveu
Los Angeles 16, Calif.

Dear John:

Things are moving along a little faster than 1 expected,1 expect
the Diamond Drill People here next Sunday and they are going to
put me on a cost price basis for the remainder of the drilling.
This will reduce the price considerable,which is a welcome sound
to me. If you feel that you can do so will you send me the balance
that 1 asked for.This will help me to finish the Drilling to the
extent that the Goverment men will take over,and they will take
their pay out of the ten percent of the ore shipped.They estimate it
cost about $6000.00 to do the necessary stripping.They also
estimate that it will take untill the first of November to start
the shipping,instead of December as 1 told you 1 thought it would
take.The Drilling has progressed faster than 1 expected and 1 will
need the balance to clear the pay roll,as the Goverment will take
over the cost plus payments.They are are very anxious to get the ore
going to the smelter as they need the Copper.

They estimate that 1 will be able to ship about 500 tons per month
by the first of the year.

1 do not think 1 can be in Los Angeles untill the 15th of November

Sincerely yours

B.T. Spalding.

Copy of Mr. B.T. Spalding letter which acknowledge having received
money from me and desiring the balance.

This, a copy of a letter written by Spalding in the last year
of his life to a business associate, conveys the depth of his
involvement in mining and related enterprises.

F. C. Box 1460
Tularcsa, New Mexico
Sept. 17th. 1952.

Dear Mr. DeVorss:

I am out here where no one knows me with only four hours of work a day and the rest of the time to working on the M.M. Also no one bothers me, and will stay until the M.M. is finished there are but few changes, but it will take me until the 20th. of next month before it will be finished. The reason I moved friends found out my location and there were constant calls.

When it is due will you kindly send the balance of the money to the Bank as per enclosed blank chack . They cash my checks readily.

Have a house to myself one half mile out and nobody bothers me.

Will keep you posted as to any change.

Sincerely

B. T. Spalding.

ALAMOGORDO, N. M. ___Tularosa Branch_____ 19___   95-105
                                                          1122

OTERO COUNTY STATE BANK

PAY TO THE
ORDER OF_____ $_____
          KNOW YOUR ENDORSER—REQUIRE IDENTIFICATION

_____ DOLLARS

FOR_____   _____

Baird Spalding to Douglas DeVorss, Sept. 17, 1952. His self-imposed isolation was fairly characteristic despite the many friends he could boast. "M.M." may be his way of referring to an MS (manuscript) or to the *Masters* (plural abbreviation, MM), i.e. Vol. 5 of *Life and Teaching*. Work on this was delayed by three deaths in the following year: Spalding's in March, DeVorss' wife's in June, and DeVorss' own in September.

Truth or Conseque
New Mexico
March 14--1953.

Dear Dug:

I came here to get rid of a bad cold and expected to
leave for Los Angeles Monday. This morning I had a
letter from Reno making me an offer on a property I
have there. Now I will go to Reno and try and despose
of the proprty which will take me a week.

Will ask that you send my check when the time comes
to Reno in cair of Allen Weyl 1254 Patrick Avenue
Reno Nevada.

Sincerely

B. T. Spalding

Baird Spalding to Douglas DeVorss four days before his
death. This is his last known communication.

LA Author, 97 Dies In Tempe Auto Court

TEMPE, March 19—Baird T. Spaulding, 97, Los Angeles, Calif., was found dead in his room yesterday at an auto court, 1820 Apache Boulevard. Efforts of Fire Chief Carl Spain to revive him with a resuscitator were futile.

RAYMOND Kalish, operator of the court, who discovered the body, said an unvented gas heater was burning in the room. Kalish said a window in the room was partly open and a resident of the court said she had seen Mr. Spaulding go to his truck and return to his room about 10 a.m.

Mr. Spaulding, world traveler, lecturer, and author, had checked into the court about midnight Tuesday. His primary vocation was that of mining engineer. After conferring with a local physician, Justice of the Peace Ralph Fowler said there would be no inquest.

AMONG HIS BOOKS is "Teachings of the Masters of the Far East," which has been translated into several languages. He had owned extensive property in Taluroosa, N. M.

Friends in Phoenix include City Magistrate C. W. Pensinger. There are no known local survivors.

Funeral services and burial are pending at Carr Mortuary.

From the *Phoenix Gazette* of March 19, 1953. Spalding's name was misspelled and his age overstated by two years.

The auto-court room — Spalding's last abode — at 1820 Apache Blvd., Tempe, Arizona; shown are proprietor Raymond Kalish (left) and Spalding's friend David Bruton (right).

Dear Doug:

I picked up the other paper from Mr. Ward at
the Probate department in the Court House.
Later, I went to the Health Department of the
State of Arizona in an effort to get the death
certificates you requested. However, I could
not get them today but they will be mailed
directly to you. It seems a few days must be
allowed to "process" a death certificate. I
stressed the urgency in this case and got a
"Please Rush" attached. You should receive
them around the first of next week.

Obtained Spalding's ashes at noon today.
They were scattered in a beautiful desert
setting in Papago Park. Had coffee with Judge
Pensinger later in the afternoon. He was
pleased with the final disposition of the ashes.

Called a W. C. Fields's office and showed the
rest of the mining papers to his secretary.
Several of them have Epitaph's name on them.
Told the secretary to tell Fields she had seen *he*
the papers and to notify their client could see
them for a limited time at Judge Fowler's office.

Delivered these papers, maps and all things pertaining to the mining business in a neat little
box to Judge Fowler and requested a receipt
for same. I told him Mr. Beatson will send for
them later.

Certainly, this winds up the Arizona affairs of
the late Baird T. Heard a couple of new tales
of his from Pensinger. There seems no end to them.

Will leave for Los Angeles in the morning (Wednesday) but may stay over in Desert Hot Springs
tomorrow night. Will call you as soon as I
arrive.

                    Sincerely,

                    DAVID BRUTON

March 24, 1953

4710 N. Central Ave.,
Phoenix, Arizona

June 24, 1953

Mrs. W. Wunderly
940 Burke Road
Balwyn, Melbourne,
Victoria, Australia

Dear Mrs. Wunderly:

Your letter addressed to Mr. Baird T. Spalding has been opened by us. As you will see from the enclosed, Mr. Spalding passed on last March 18, at Tempe, Arizona.

Mr. DeVorss was appointed sole beneficiary and participated in the memorial services on March 22.

We are very happy to learn that you have derived so much benefit from the four volumes LIFE & TEACHING OF THE MASTERS OF THE FAR EAST, and were Mr. Spalding alive we feel sure he would answer your letter personally. Since he is no longer in physical embodiment, we feel sure by re-reading and studying his books, you will find the answer to your questions, as so many thousands of others have.

Mr. Spalding, in his numerous lectures, always said - "Man gives 90% of his time to negative thoughts and expressions and only 10% to constructive and positive thoughts and expressions." And again: "If we would only see every person as a Master right now, and not see the shortcomings of the individual."

Perhaps more than any other person we know, Mr. Spalding practiced the law of omnipresent supply, for no sooner was he in receipt of a sum of money, large or small, than he immediately turned it over to someone in need. He never kept anything for himself; he never thought of himself, but always of being the living Presence at all times. He actually lived in that higher consciousness as taught in his books.

We thank you for your expressions of love and gratitude to Mr. Spalding, and feel sure that with your continued study and application help and illumination and guidance will be yours.

Sincerely yours,
DEVORSS & CO.

AMW·s

DeVorss & Company tried to answer as many "fan" letters to Spalding as it could after his death. The world was slow to learn of his passing. These observations make a fitting tribute.